The Journey to Oregon – 1934

The true story of eight family members who move
from Nebraska to Oregon
in August 1934
in search of a better life.

A Novella

By

Jean Braden

The Journey to Oregon – 1934 is based on actual events. I dramatized interactions and conversations to tell the story.

Cover design by Will Bruno
Interior design by Erika Wong

Dedicated to my mother
Helen Marie Schafer
and my aunts
Helen Gesina Maria Lichty
and
Ella Scharff Schafer

Acknowledgements

I was raised with the oral history of my family's move to Oregon in 1934. The written story started taking shape in a memoir class taught by Ariel Gore at The Attic in Portland, Oregon. Ariel helped me with the structure and flow of the story.

Along with his love and encouragement Gary, my husband, drove me hundreds of miles to help with my research. He drove me all over Nebraska and we followed the old Highway 30 from Nebraska to Oregon. He also drove me up and down the Historic Columbia River Scenic Highway several different times.

My daughter, Sarah, had faith that I would be able to complete this project and her support and encouragement included reading, scanning, and printing the manuscript as well as walking the Twin Tunnels with me.

The members of the Out of the Attic writing group—Asha, Linda, Liv, Lori, Jackie, Jan, Lainie, Margaret, Sarah and Tiffany—provided input and support throughout the entire project.

Thanks to all of you!

Jean

Left to Right: George, John, Harmon, Helen, Ella, Mary, Bill, Gesina – in Oregon, 1935

The Journey to Oregon – 1934

Family members making the trip to Oregon include:
John Schafer (age 24)
Helen Fiedler Schafer (17), John's wife of six months.

John's parents
Harmon Schafer (51)
Mary Varwig Schafer (43)

John's siblings
Bill Schafer (21)
Ella Scharff Schafer (21), Bill's wife of one year
George Schafer (16)
Gesina Schafer (12)

Helen leaned heavily on her walker as she moved across the floor of her studio apartment and slowly settled into her recliner. Jean followed her into the room. "What a nice eighty-eighth birthday party, Mom, but I bet you're tired."

"Now, how many people were there?" Helen asked as she pulled up the footrest on her chair.

"Well, let's see, you have three children, eight grandchildren, twelve great grandchildren, and five great-great grandchildren. They all came, so that's twenty-eight. Plus everyone's spouses or significant others, and other family and friends. It was quite a large gathering. What are you grinning about?"

Helen's smile was soft and happy. "Your Dad always used to say to me, 'Mom, look what we started.'"

"Yes, I remember," Jean chuckled as she leaned over and tucked an afghan around her mother's legs. "I'll leave your gifts here on the counter with a list of who gave you what. You just go ahead and take a rest."

Helen leaned her head back on the chair and closed her eyes. She loved her family, but it was draining when everyone was around. She felt Jean lean over and give her a light kiss. "Love you, Mom. I'll talk to you later."

"Love you, too," Helen muttered as she drifted off, feeling light and airy. She felt her body begin to float into the air and slowly drift above the clouds. She was high in the sky, but she could also see everything on earth below her. She drifted by the house on 48th Avenue in Salem where she and Johnny had lived after they sold the farm. She floated over the farm on Schafer Avenue where they had raised their children. She moved east across the country, over the Cascades, Salt Lake, and the Rocky Mountains, and finally back to the plains of Nebraska. She drifted closer to the ground and when she squinted her eyes, she could see the house in Lexington where she'd grown up. A little farther to the east she could see the city of Kearney, and below her, the farmhouse where she and Johnny lived for the first six months of their marriage.

She seemed to hover over the farm. Grasshoppers chirped as they ate the dead corn stalks. The earth was dry and cracked, and in the distance she could see dirt as it whirled into dust clouds. As she drifted closer to the farm, she could see a few cottonwood trees around the house. Their tops were brown and it looked like they were dying.

As she floated still closer to the earth, she saw three people in the yard of the farmhouse and, on the road headed to the house, a car with dust flying behind it.

That looks like Johnny and me. Who's that with us? Helen rubbed her eyes to get a better look. *Why, it's George. Looks like we're getting ready to eat lunch. The table is set up under the tree in the yard.* She slowly slipped into the body of the seventeen-year-old woman in the yard.

John and his 1930 Ford Tudor

John, Helen, and John's younger brother, George, were just sitting down to eat at the table in the sparse shade of the tree when they heard a car approach. As the dust cloud moved toward them, Helen grabbed a tablecloth from the clothesline and spread it over the food to keep the dust off their lunch.

Thank goodness I have enough food for another person, Helen thought as the car pulled into the yard. Luckily she had baked bread and made noodles, and she had gravy from the canned beef she was serving. She had taken cottage cheese from the bag that hung on the clothesline and there was fresh buttermilk and butter made from their cow's milk.

Even though she still watered the garden a couple times a day, it had shriveled because of the drought and the extreme heat. She carried a bucket of water and dipped into it using a large ladle. The well was deep and gave enough water for the house, the garden and the large watering trough for the cow and goat. She had canned several quarts of pickles and later this fall they would dig potatoes and pick squash. She was worried about having enough food to last through the winter. *It's so hot* Helen thought. Her dress stuck to her body and sweat ran down her back and between her breasts.

John stood up, frowning, as the 1928 Oldsmobile Whippet came to a stop. "Why, it's Bill. What's he doin' driving this far in the middle of the week?" Helen just shrugged.

Pal, the six-month-old St. Bernard, barked and ran to the car, his big paws stirring up the dust. The car door slammed and Bill bent down and patted Pal, then walked toward the trio at the table, wiping his head with his handkerchief. "Man, it's hot. When I went through town it was already over 102 degrees and they guessed it would get to 108 today!"

John met him halfway and slapped his younger brother on the back. "You're just in time for lunch – the folks okay?"

"Yes, everyone's fine, but I want to talk to you about something."

"Hi, Bill. Come and sit down, let me get another plate," Helen said.

After a friendly punch to Bill's shoulder, George headed to the house. "I'll get a chair."

Helen observed the three brothers as she carried a plate for Bill. They all had dark hair combed straight back over their heads and they were all very thin. When they talked they used the same words and vocal pitches. Even their laughter sounded alike. They were all within an inch or two in height, but Bill was the tallest. George, who was sixteen, had been boarding with them for the last six weeks while working for a farmer down the road.

"What brings you here on a Tuesday?" John asked Bill as they started eating. Pal lay quietly under the table waiting for the leftovers. The cottonwood tree the table sat under was slowly dying because of the drought, but it provided shade and it was a little cooler than being in the direct sun or in the house. At night, they brought their mattresses outside to sleep under it.

"I wrote to Aunt Dora and Uncle Mick in Oregon a few weeks ago asking them if there was any work there. I just got a letter back and they said there's plenty of work and they would help us find housing and jobs if we came out," Bill said as he salted his noodles and gravy.

"Why'd you write to 'em asking about work?" John took a bite of meat.

"Cause there ain't any work here. I haven't been able to find any work for the last few months and they won't let Ella teach next year 'cause we're married. We lived apart for nine months so she could finish the teaching year, but we want to be together now, in our own place, not living with Mom and Dad." Bill wiped up the gravy on his plate with his bread. "Mom and Dad had a bad year, the corn is only about two feet tall and burned - can't even use it for fodder."

"Yeah, same thing's happen' here." John sipped his cold tea.

"Helen, would you pass the tomatoes?" George asked, keeping his eyes on Bill.

"When Dad thrashed the wheat he only got five bushels per acre, which paid out at only ten cents a bushel."

"Let's see, at three thousand two hundred fifty bushels from the six hundred fifty acres of wheat…" John pulled a pencil stub from one pocket of his overalls and a piece of paper from another. "That comes to about three hundred twenty-five dollars for the season. That ain't enough to pay the farm rent." He frowned looking up at Bill.

"Right. So I wrote back to Aunt Dora that we're coming. We're packin' up and leavin' for Oregon this Saturday, August 11th. Do you and Helen want to come along?"

There was silence at the table. John and Helen looked at each other, astonished.

"Who's we?" John asked.

"Mom, Dad, Gesina, Ella and me."

"How long do you think it'll take to drive?"

"I've thought about this a lot," Bill said, brushing his dark hair back away from his face. "Ella and I looked at the map and figure it's about eighteen hundred miles, more or less. I think we'd be able to do it in five or six days, if we can average forty miles an hour. Do you think we could average that?" Bill looked at his older brother.

"I'd guess that'd be a good average, considering you're going through the mountains." John scratched his head.

"We'll camp at night so there won't be the expense of paying for somewhere to sleep. Dad'll sell what cows he can, the horse and buggy, and they'll sell their furniture and other farm things too, so he'll be able to buy a used truck to drive to Oregon."

"Well, I'm not staying here if everyone else is going." George shook his head. "I'll go get my money from Mr. Sims right now. Then I'll go back with you today to help the folks pack up. I've been working for fifty cents a day for the last six weeks, so he owes me twenty-one bucks."

"I'll drive you over. Then we'll come back and get your things," Bill offered. "Dad'll be able to use your help with the sale. When we get back here maybe John and Helen will have decided if they want to go with us."

As the car left the yard, John and Helen remained at the table looking at one another.

"What do you think?" Helen asked John. Her dark hair fell into her thin face.

"I'm tired of working hard and having nothing to show for it. We aren't goin' to have enough money to pay all the rent to your Mom. Maybe it'd be good to go somewhere else. Dora and Mick have been in Oregon for several years and have done good. If we go, we won't be out there on our own."

"Well, I'm going wherever you're goin'," Helen smiled. A slow glow settled over her as she looked at her handsome husband. They had only been married six months and she was so in love with him.

"Won't you miss your Mom and your brothers?" John speared the last slice of tomato from the plate and salted it before he ate it.

"Yes, I will. But I can't stay here just because of them. Dick is still living with Mom until he finishes high school. Elmer and Bob are in the military, and come home once a year on leave. Besides, I'm married now, and I need to be with my husband."

John rose from the table and gave her a kiss. "Well, it's settled then." He picked up his straw hat from the end of the table and headed to the barn. He wore overalls over his blue shirt and they were both stained under the arms and down the back.

Helen cleared the table and tossed the scraps to the dog. Pal's tail wagged back and forth as he ate. He had been a wedding gift and she really enjoyed having him around; the only problem was trying to fill him up. She glanced at the barn and saw the hens, also a wedding gift, pecking in the barnyard. She would feed them later and collect the eggs. Billy, the goat, and Betty, the cow, were at the water trough. She smiled as she remembered the time Billy had chased Gesina, John's twelve-year-old sister, up the ladder into the cherry tree, and then climbed the ladder behind her. Gesina had screamed at the top of her lungs.

Helen put the buttermilk, butter and meat in the cool area under the porch. She and Johnny would have a cold supper tonight, probably bread and milk. It would be too hot to use the stove. She washed the dishes on the porch with the hot water that she heated on the back of the wood stove. As she worked, her mind began to wander back to the time she first met Johnny.

Her older brother, Bob, had played baseball with a group of men in Lexington and one day he brought Johnny home after a game. Bob introduced him to Helen and that was that. They kept company for a year before they got married. She had wanted to finish her senior year of school, but they got married on February 28, 1934, just four months shy of graduation. As a married woman she wasn't allowed to attend school. She was sixteen and Johnny was twenty-three when they married.

Farms were rented on March 1, the beginning of each work season. They had struggled to raise a crop these last five months, but in spite of their hard work nothing was growing. The dust and drought killed the wheat and corn crops, so Johnny worked for other farmers whenever he could to make some money. It would be hard to leave her mother, who was working as a housekeeper in Kearney. She knew she'd miss her three brothers, too, but she was married to Johnny and would go where he led.

* * * * *

Standing in the doorway of the barn, John took off his straw hat, brushed the dark hair out of his blue eyes, and watched Helen on the porch. He was ready for a change; he was tired of the heat and the dust. Even though he worked hard, he hadn't been able to make any money with the drought and dust storms of the last several years. He'd always worked for someone else and it felt like he'd never be able to own anything at this rate. John rubbed the back of his neck, it was tight with tension. Moving to Oregon would be a big change. They wouldn't have enough money to come back if Oregon didn't work out, but they had to take that risk; there wasn't anything for them here. His mind was busy with the things he'd have to do. He would need to talk with Helen's mom, Lurena, who was aware of the crop situation, and who probably wouldn't be surprised by their decision to leave. He would see Mr. Sarnes and his son, Lowell, to collect the money they each owed him.

Thank goodness the 1930 Ford Tudor was a reliable car. He grinned as he recalled the ad that appeared in the Dawson County Pioneer newspaper on August 8, 1930.

> *Have you had a ride? Come in or phone 107 and we will give you a Free Ride in one of our New Ford Demonstrators – You can drive it yourself - we want you to – so that you will know how comfortable it rides. We are giving away FREE a NEW FORD TUDOR on August 22 at the Dawson County Fair. Get your name in the pot, you may be the one to get it. Only 14 more days left to get your demonstration."*
>
> *Lexington Motor Company*
> *Lexington, Nebraska*

He'd made sure to get to the fairgrounds and drove that car around the racetrack, then put his name into the drawing. He was working in the cornfield when his friend came running down the row yelling that he had won. He had ruined his straw hat by jumping up and down on it in his excitement. He immediately went to town to pick up the car, grinning all the way.

On August 29, 1930, the Dawson County Pioneer Newspaper reported:

Schafer Won Ford

"A new Ford Tudor given away on Friday at the County Fair by the Lexington Motor Company went to John Schafer, a young man 20 years of age, who came here about six months ago from Upland, Nebraska, and who is employed by Julius Van Butsell, a farmer living one mile north of Lexington. The number that won the car was 1881 and there were 2028 numbers in the tin box."

The car was easy to drive and ran well. He'd never had any problems with it, so he was sure it would make it to Oregon. Maybe he would pull a trailer along behind, but he'd heard other people say you couldn't pull a trailer over the Rocky Mountains. *I'll have to think about that,* he frowned. He and Helen didn't have a lot of things anyway, so they'd just pack what they couldn't sell.

He looked at Helen and smiled. She was thin and as tall as he was with dark hair that lay close around her face. She smiled with eyes that sparkled when she laughed, which was often. She was always ready for a challenge and she'd be a good sport about this change. Together they'd make a new and better life in Oregon. They both knew how to work hard and how to manage with little or no money. With a new spring in his step, he went back into the barn to put down Russian thistles for the cow that would come in later for milking.

* * * * *

When Bill and George returned, George jumped out of the car, red faced, and swinging his arms. He stomped over to where John and Helen stood. "I'm so mad, Mr. Sims doesn't have any money to pay me. He has eighteen cows and he was supposed to milk half and I would milk half, but then he had sunstroke and was unable to do any work. I did it all.

He has fourteen horses and one hundred fifty hogs. I've been mowing Russian thistles for feed because there ain't any hay. My day started at 4:30am and ended about 8pm. Six weeks of work for nothin'. I guess he'll have to do all the work now! I can't wait to go."

He stomped into the house to get his belongings and when he returned he threw them into the trunk of Bill's car. John and Bill made plans on where to meet and what to take.

As they drove out of the yard, John stood with his arm around Helen as they waved goodbye. Pal sat beside them, tongue hanging out and panting. "We'll meet 'em about 10am in Kearney on Saturday. That's four days from now. We've got a lot to do before we're ready to leave. You still sure you want to go?"

"Yes…yes. I'll be ready." Helen leaned her head on his shoulder.

John and Helen's Wedding Photo – February 28, 1934

AUGUST 9, 1934

John drove the car from the barn to the house with the trailer attached. The chickens were in a cage in the trailer and Billy, the goat, was tied into the trailer as well. John got out of the car in front of the house where Helen was petting Pal.

"I'd best be goin' as the sale starts about 10am," he said.

"Yes, I know." Tears streamed down Helen's face.

John picked up the string that went to Pal's collar. "Come on, boy." John turned and hugged Helen. "I'll find him a good home."

Helen wiped her eyes as she hugged Pal goodbye, but she also had to laugh, because Pal sat in the front seat just like a person, happy to be going for a ride. Pal was a wedding gift from Mr. and Mrs. Juhl, neighbors of her family in Lexington. Bud, Pal's sire, was a big lumbering full bred St. Bernard who had always loved to play with Helen and her younger brother Dick. When the pond in town froze over Helen would throw a tin can onto the pond and Bud would chase it. Helen would grab hold of the dog's tail, Dick would hold onto Helen, and away they would fly across the pond. She missed Pal already, but they just couldn't take him. The vehicles would be crowded with family, and there would be no place for him to ride. He took up a lot of room and ate a lot. It would be hard enough to keep themselves fed on the trip with what little food they were taking.

Helen returned to the house to resume packing. Dust covered the dishes in the cupboard and they all had to be cleaned before she packed them. She shook out the clothing - everything was covered with the dust that blew through the house. Using newspaper, she wrapped up every-thing that was to be sent later - the beautiful bowls, plates and cut glass dishes they'd received as wedding gifts. She especially loved the six long-stemmed etched green water glasses that Aunt Mae had given them, and the clear glass bowl with sauce dishes and gold trim that had been given to John when he was born.

She had to leave the doll carriage she received at Christmas when she was ten, the large doll she bought with her first babysitting money when she was twelve, and the doll cradle that her Dad had made her. Helen remembered when her father was building the cradle, and when she asked what he was making, he told her a ladder for the cat. She had been thrilled to find the cradle under the Christmas tree that year.

Her father, George Michael Fiedler, had been the supervisor of the Department of Commerce Emergency Landing Field at the airstrip in Lexington. He died of a ruptured ulcer and *peritonitis* when she was thir-teen. *He loved to tell stories and play jokes on everyone. He always made me laugh. I miss him so much; he would have been excited about our trip.*

Everything they left behind would be stored here at the farmhouse because her Mom, Lurena Marshall Fiedler, and Dick, her thirteen-year-old brother, were planning to move back into the house once she and John left. When they got settled in Oregon, they would have their things sent out.

Glancing around the room she saw her violin lying on the top of the piano. The violin and piano always went together at their house.

When Mom played the piano, Dad accompanied her on the violin. The house sang with their music. They met when George played the violin and Lurena played the piano at Lurena's cousin's wedding. Her father's violin was passed on to her brother Bob, but this violin was hers. It had belonged to her grandfather. As a child she asked him if she could try to learn to play, and he'd let her. When she played in the high school orchestra, he told her she could have it. Her mom would later send the violin along with her other treasures.

She blinked and realized she'd been daydreaming. At the bottom of the steamer trunk she put their winter boots, overcoats, and winter clothes, a layer of tissue paper, then John's suit and her wedding dress. Her Mom had bought the dress for her; the blouse was a pale blue patterned print and the attached skirt was gray. The vest-style top was gray and criss-crossed over the blouse and buttoned onto the skirt. Her mom had also gotten her a pair of two-inch heels of blended shades of gray. *I always feel so elegant when I wear my dress and shoes.* She looked at her thin gold wedding band and smiled as she remembered their wedding.

The day was cold and sunny, with snow piled on the sidewalks and streets. It was Wednesday, and Reverend Bert Storey conducted the service at the Kearney Methodist parsonage. Helen's Mom, her brothers Dick and Bob, and Gladys White, her best friend, came. Elmer, her oldest brother, was in the Army and couldn't come. Bob was the best man and Gladys was the maid-of-honor. John's family wasn't there, as they couldn't come in the middle of the week. Bill was working and Dad Schafer only drove short distances. After the wedding, everyone gathered at Uncle Guy and Aunt Mae's for a lovely supper. Aunt Mae, her Mom's sister, made a beautiful angel food wedding cake. Gladys came back to the farm with Helen and John and spent the night with them before heading home the next day.

Gladys was nineteen, a widow with a baby boy, and was living back at home with her parents. Gladys and Henry had been married less than a year when he fell from the barn roof and died. *Gladys always looks so sad,* Helen thought. *It must really be hard for her not having Henry around, especially with a new baby. I'm so lucky to have Johnny.*

On top of the wedding clothes and a layer of tissue paper, Helen laid the wedding ring quilt Grandma Fiedler had made for her. Then she added their bedding and towels. On the top she placed her small baby doll that she had gotten with the doll carriage, and, lastly, their wedding picture.

In the suitcase she packed her extra summer dress and the overalls, shirt, and shoes she wore when working in the fields, John's extra set of overalls and a shirt, and their extra underwear and socks. The suitcase would sit on the back seat of the car, while the trunk would go into the bed of the truck. Along the way they'd eat the dill pickles, chokecherry jam, and the beef she had canned. She also packed two sets of plates, cups, glasses, and silverware.

She had just finished when she heard the car drive into the yard. It was almost 4 o'clock and she hadn't even thought about eating lunch. She'd fix supper after awhile.

John smiled as he walked across the room toward her and slapped his straw hat on his leg. "There was a real nice family that was lookin' for a good work dog and they liked Pal. They gave me two dollars for him. They have four children and Pal was gentle with them already. I think he'll be happy."

"That's good. Did you sell the animals and the trailer?"

"Yep, sold everything. We didn't make much, but at least it's somethin'. With the seventy-five dollars Mr. Sarnes paid me, we should have enough for the trip. Too bad Lowell didn't have any money for me, but he didn't have any crops, either." John put his hat on the table, leaned over and hugged her. "How'd your day go?"

"I sorted and packed up all the wedding gifts that will stay here and packed all our clothes to take with us. What food we don't take we can leave for Mom." Helen brushed the hair out of her eyes. "Can you help me move the boxes of stuff we're leaving here into the second bedroom so they'll be out of Mom's way?"

"Sure, then I'll do the milkin' and finish up the barn chores."

"Is a cold supper okay with you?"

"Just fix whatever's easy."

After they had eaten they sat on the porch steps and watched the fireflies flit around the yard. The stars were beginning to fill the sky above the layer of dust that floated in the air. The evening was still hot and muggy, but a breeze moved the air around them. Dustdevils skipped across the dirt in the yard.

"It'll be strange to live somewhere else; Nebraska has always been my home," Helen sighed. She laid her head on John's shoulder. "Do you think we'll like it in Oregon?"

"Guess we'll have to. We won't have enough money to come back." John put his arm around her. "Well, tomorrow we'll help your mom move back here to the farm."

"Uh-huh. At least all she and Dick have to move is their clothes. All the furniture is here." Helen gazed off into the distance. "I've written to Elmer and Bob about going to Oregon, but since they're in the Army, they probably haven't received my letters yet. It worries me that I don't have an address for George and Irene. I hate for us to leave without letting our best friends know. Have you heard anything about where George found work?"

John shook his head. "No, but we can always write to George's folks once we're settled in Oregon and they'll pass on where we're at."

"Yes." Helen bit her lip. "That would work. You know, Johnny, I'm a little worried about traveling all the way to Oregon with your family."

"Why?" John pushed the dark hair off her forehead, and lightly brushed his fingers across her mouth.

"Well, for one, Bill always wants to do things his way and often won't listen to others."

John's blue eyes twinkled with laughter. "You just need to know how to handle him, and no one knows how to do that better than his big brother. Don't worry. Decisions will be made with everyone getting a chance to say how they feel. What else?"

"Well, Gesina is twelve years old and she and I have a little sister/ big sister relationship and that's no problem. And George is just like a younger brother to me, we get along fine." Helen looked him in the eye. "But what I really worry about is your mom. She doesn't like me. I don't do things right from her point of view, and then your dad never talks to me. How am I going to be able to travel all the way to Oregon with them?"

"Don't let Ma bother you, that's just her way. She's that way with everyone, even me. I just ignore it. Don't worry about dad, either. He's always quiet and rarely talks with anyone. Together, you and I will be able to handle anything. Just tell me if something is bothering you." John caressed the back of her neck.

They sat quietly for a few minutes, each lost in their own thoughts.

"I hope my family will come to visit us." Helen's hazel eyes turned soft. "I'll sure miss them."

"They probably will; they might even move to Oregon someday." John kissed her gently.

"Do you think so?"

"Never can tell. I know you'll miss your mom and brothers. I promise to bring you back to Nebraska for a visit sometime."

"Really? That would be wonderful."

"You'll see, Helen. We'll be back." Arms around each other, they headed inside.

The group stood in the yard of Mary and Harmon's empty house outside Upland. It was late afternoon by the time the truck was finally loaded. It had been a fast-paced five days since they decided to go to Oregon. Clothes stuck to everyone and faces shone with perspiration. Bill stood with his arm around Ella. George was standing a little off to the side. Harmon and Mary, the parents of John, Bill, George and Gesina, stood together, and Gesina stood next to Ella.

"The house sure looks small, now that it's empty, doesn't it?" Bill asked. He removed his hat and rubbed his head with his hand.

"I know." Ella shaded her eyes with her hand and looked back at the barn. "Even the barn looks small and it seems to be leaning."

"That's cause there ain't no animals in the barn anymore." George's eyes were suspiciously bright.

Ella glanced back at the barn. Her eyes fell to the dirt that looked almost black under the destroyed stalks of corn and wheat in the fields. The trees were all dead and the dirt blew freely across the fields and yard. By the barn you could see where Mary dumped the extra milk they didn't use. John and Bill had tried to talk their parents into feeding the extra milk to the hogs, but to no avail.

Harmon looked off over the fields. His once tall, straight body and long stride had changed to slumped shoulders and a shuffling walk. Life on the farm was always hard, but this year had been especially bad. He didn't have enough money to pay rent for the year. What little money he'd saved was lost when the banks failed. He'd decided to go to Oregon with John and Bill. He sold all his machinery, six horses, eight cows and a bunch of hogs. He also sold his Model T. Ford, which he only drove to town and to church, his buggy, lumber wagons and all the furniture except for what was on the truck. They'd held a farm sale, but no one bought anything so he sold everything to a dealer in Kearney. He'd received $450 for everything, and then bought a truck for $200 for the trip which either John or Bill would drive. He hoped $250 would get them to Oregon. *It'll be hard to leave my brothers. I sure will miss 'em,* he thought.

Mary, Harmon's wife, was short, and her graying hair was pulled into a tight bun at the top of her head. She didn't want to start over in Oregon, but she and Harmon couldn't manage the farm without help from the boys. *At least we're goin' to family,* she thought. *My sister, Dora, says we can find work there, hope she's right. Things have to be better there, and perhaps Harmon can find work. He's been a failure here, couldn't even get enough of a crop to pay rent on the farm.* Mary's face looked grim.

Ella stepped forward and put her arm around Gesina. "Don't cry, Gesina. It'll be okay." Ella was only a few inches taller than Mary, and Gesina didn't come up to her chin yet. She was a thin child with long dark hair that hid most of her face. Her twelve-year-old eyes were red from weeping.

"No, it won't." Gesina wiped her hazel eyes. "I'm leaving everything and I don't know anybody where we're going. And Oregon is so far away. I want to stay here and start school next month with my friends."

"I know how hard it is to think of moving away and having to leave everything here. Bill and I have to do it, too," Ella said.

"But you *want* to go. I don't. I don't know why Mom and Dad are leaving."

"Gesina," Bill said, biting off his words. "We've talked about this several times already. The folks can't pay the rent 'cause there weren't no crops. They'd have to move off the farm, anyway. Nothing would be the same."

"But if we had moved to another farm I could take my things with me. This way I had to sell everything."

"Gesina, I'm sorry. Tell me again what you had to sell." Ella's arm tightened around Gesina and she brought Gesina closer to her.

Gesina sniffled and blew her nose. "I had to sell my special doll that I got for Christmas, my doll buggy, and the pump organ that Mom and Dad got me. And the table, chairs and cupboard that Bill made for me that I played with in the old corncrib. And I don't even get to tell my friends *good-bye*. They don't know I'm leaving." She started to cry harder.

"Gesina, stop blubbering." Her mother strode over to where Gesina stood next to Ella. "Now, get into the truck quickly. Fast, Gesina, fast." Mary pushed Gesina along with her hand to move her toward the truck. Gesina scrambled into the vehicle.

The truck was loaded with Harmon and Mary's things: three mattresses, a bedstead, and Bill and Ella's trunk and mattress. There was also clothing, food and a table.

Bill climbed into the driver's seat in the cab of the truck, and Harmon and Gesina rode with him. Ella got in their 1928 Whippet, and Mary and George joined her. Bill and Ella had their clothes in the car as well as two fifty-pound bags of flour. There was just enough room in the back for George. *I hope our forty dollars lasts till we get to Oregon,* Ella thought.

They drove to Upland, about six miles from their farm, to spend the night with Henry Schafer, one of Harmon's brothers.

"Hey, what's going on?" Henry called to the group as they pulled in to the yard.

"We're head'n for Oregon," Bill said.

"You are? For heavens sakes, I didn't know you were goin'," Henry said. He stumbled a couple of steps backward, surprised at the news. "When did you decide to go to Oregon? I didn't know you were thinkin' about it."

"We decided just this past Monday. We had a farm sale and got rid of everything."

"Why can't you stay? The government will buy your stock," Henry said, turning to talk to his older brother.

"I ain't letting nobody shoot my animals and bury 'em in the ground. I sold 'em to a dealer," Harmon said.

"Well, heck, he'll probably just sell 'em to the government. You might as well have gotten the money," Henry said.

"Nope, not shootin' my animals." Harmon gave his brother a pat on the back.

"We hoped to spend the night with you all before we leave in the mornin' to meet John and Helen in Kearney."

"John's going with you, too?"

"Yep. They don't have no crops this year, either."

"Guess Mary will let the missus know your plans; we'll be glad to have you stay with us tonight," Henry said. The two men started walking down to the barn. "George, come along, I can use your help," Henry called.

George ran and caught up with the two men, who were the same height and walked with the same gait.

AUGUST 11, 1934

I t was early when they left Henry's place. They had a good feed of eggs and bacon before starting out. Bill drove the truck and led the way with Ella following. Henry and his wife, Lena, stood in the yard waving good-bye to them.

"I hope Oregon will be good for Harmon. He seems unhappy and doesn't walk with pride like he used to." Henry squinted his eyes through the dust and watched the vehicles drive through the two blocks of town.

"Mary's really nervous about traveling to Oregon. It's hard for her to leave her home, all her family and all her things. At forty-three it's hard to have to start over with no idea what will be ahead." Lena used her apron to brush the dust away from her face. "I hope they have a good trip and a good life in Oregon."

"They're lucky to have all their children going with 'em," Henry said.

They turned back to the yard. Henry went to the barn and Lena walked toward the house.

* * * * *

George's bicycle was tied on the back of the truck and eight solid maple kitchen chairs hung four to a side on the rack around the outside of the truck. They had almost reached Minden, Nebraska, when the bottom fell off one of the chairs. Ella tooted the horn and Bill stopped. The solid maple chairs were shaken to pieces, so they stopped at a secondhand store to sell them.

"Well, I'll give you one dollar for all the chairs, but I won't buy them unless you also sell me the bicycle for two dollars," the dealer said.

"Mom, I don't want to sell my bicycle." George slapped his leg with his hand. "That's how I get around."

"You have to. We've got to sell the chairs, so you've got to sell your bicycle." As Mary walked over to Harmon, the wind caught her dress and the tops of her black shoes showed. Mary took off her straw hat and fanned herself with it. After she pushed it back onto her head, she nodded.

* * * * *

John and Helen were standing by the car, just south of Kearney, where Highway 30 connected with the road from Upland. It was 10 o'clock. They had expected the others to already be there.

"I wonder why they're not here yet," Helen said. She blew her nose and rubbed her eyes. Saying good-bye to her Mom and Dick that morning had been hard. She felt shaky and nervous, with butterflies fluttering in her stomach. She wasn't sure if going to Oregon was such a good idea, after all.

At least they were wearing clean clothes. She had washed yesterday and ironed last night. John's blue shirt and overalls looked good on him. He also wore heavy work boots. *He's so handsome,* Helen thought. She swirled the full skirt of her pink summer dress. She hoped her full-length cotton slip wouldn't get too hot. Rayon stockings were rolled above her knees and held in place with a band. Black tie-up shoes covered her feet.

"Maybe they started late or had some truck trouble. They'll be along soon," John replied. He removed his straw hat. One hand shaded his eyes as he gazed down the road. In the distance he could see a large dust cloud. "Maybe that's them comin' now." The gravel road was covered with dust. The dirt swirled and drifted along the fence posts, much like snow in the winter.

John filled the 1930 Ford Tudor with gas that morning when they'd driven through town. Gas cost twenty cents a gallon. He'd also gotten a couple quarts of oil just in case they needed it on the trip. *I wonder how much gas and oil will cost along the way. I hope we have enough money to make it to Oregon and to tide us over 'til we find work,* John thought. *We'll just have to be careful.* As the dust cloud came closer, John could make out an old truck, with a car following behind.

"Looks like that's 'em," he called to Helen. He strode over to her and put his arm around her shoulders. Helen covered her mouth and nose with her hand as the truck and car came to a stop. The dust swirled over everything.

When the dust finally settled, John walked over to the driver's window of the truck. "Do you want to start right off or stop for a bit?" he asked Bill.

"Let's get goin'. When we stop for lunch we can put your things into the truck. We filled a couple containers with gas, so we won't run out." Bill leaned his elbow on the window of the truck. "John, why don't you go ahead and lead the way, I'll follow and Ella can come along behind."

Before John and Helen got in the car, John reached under the seat, took an old towel and wiped the dust off the front seats, steering wheel, and gearshift. The three vehicles and eight people started down Highway 30 toward Oregon.

Driving in front we don't have to deal with the dust, Helen thought. *Here we are, on our way, headed west.*

John glanced over at Helen. "How ya doin'?"

"Okay. At least this part of the trip is familiar. I wonder how many times we've driven this road?" A smile filled with memories graced Helen's face.

"Many, many times," John replied. "The road will be familiar for another hundred miles or so."

Helen's window was rolled down, and with the wing window open, the flow of the wind into the car was controlled enough to give some air movement. She wiped her damp brow. She looked out across the field and was mesmerized by the unending barren landscape. In town you didn't notice the flatness of the prairies because there are houses and trees to break your view, but here it went on forever, just like the road goes on forever, vanishing in the distance to a pinpoint.

They drove for about thirty-five miles and were just outside of Lexington when Bill honked the horn of the truck. Helen was hungry and hoped they were stopping for lunch.

John glanced in the rear view mirror and pulled to the side of the road. Bill pulled in behind him. John grabbed his straw hat, opened the door and went back to talk with Bill. Helen twisted around, putting her arm on the back of her seat so she could watch them. Bill got out of the truck and the two men raised the hood of the truck. Steam spewed out. She watched as they got a bottle of water hanging on the side of the truck and filled the radiator.

"Looks like the radiator sprung a leak." John returned to the car with some rope. "We need to go back to Kearney to where they bought the truck and get it fixed."

"What? Go back? Can't we get it fixed in Lexington?"

"Nope. Bill can get it fixed for nothin' in Kearney. We'll stop and add water ever so often. We'll be able to get back there okay; I'll tow him if I have to."

"Is Ella driving back, too?"

"Yep, not sure how long it will take to fix." John tossed the rope into the back seat and slid into the driver's seat. "We'll eat lunch in Kearney while we wait."

Helen frowned as they turned and headed back to Kearney, going east.

* * * * *

John and Bill drove back toward the group that was waiting for them just outside of Kearney. Before they took the truck to the car dealer, they had unpacked enough food for lunch. As the car came to a stop the dust swirled around it and settled on the hood.

"What'd they say?" George ran up to the car.

"It probably won't be ready until sometime tomorrow afternoon," Bill said, talking loudly enough so everyone could hear.

"No way! You mean we have to wait here for a whole day?" George asked. He hopped on one foot, and then the other, unable to contain his disappointment.

"Yep, can't do nothin' about it. They need to get a part from Lincoln. They called and somebody will deliver it tomorrow morning. Won't take long to fix after they get the part. Have you all eaten?" Bill asked.

"Yep, but the girls made you both sandwiches," George said. "So where are we going to stay tonight, what'll we do about supper and breakfast then?" He walked along with Bill and John toward the group sitting in the shade of an abandoned filling station.

"Dad, you and Ma okay with staying here tonight? We have a little shade and water available," John said.

Harmon turned to his wife. "Guess it's okay, what'd you think, Mary?"

"I suppose it's as good as any place, since we can't go on," Mary said.

"I'll drive you and the girls over to the truck to get what food we need for supper and breakfast and the sleeping things, after it cools off a bit," John said. He flopped down beside Helen. "Do you have a sandwich for me?" he asked, giving her a big smile.

"Yes, it's here. We saved you and Bill the sardines with worms in them," she laughed, handing him the sandwich. "Do you want some water?"

"Yeah, that'll help wash down the worms!" John laughed.

Bill took a sandwich from Ella and looked at his mother. "Ma, I bought a two burner kerosene stove and a tent at the hardware store. I paid five dollars for 'em but figured they would come in handy on the road." Bill took a big bite from his sandwich. "They're in John's car; I'll get them in a bit. Also picked up some kerosene."

"It'll be easier to use the stove than having to cook over a fire," Mary nodded.

"Dad, can you pay me back? Ella and I have so little money that we can only buy gas," Bill asked. Harmon put his hand into his overall pocket and pulled out his wallet and handed Bill some one-dollar bills.

John took a big drink of water. "Helen, if you want we can go back to the farm and spend the night with your Mom. We could sleep on a bed, instead of just the mattress."

Helen's eyes opened wide but she was quiet for a moment. "No, I think I want to stay here. It was hard enough saying good-bye this morning; I don't want to have to do it all over again tomorrow."

"Okay with me."

"John," Bill called while he chewed his sandwich. "I forgot to tell you. We spent the night at Uncle Henry's last night in Upland. When I walked to the store I ran into George Loschen. He and Irene are living in town there. I told 'em you and Helen are going to Oregon with us. He hadn't heard yet and was surprised. I told him you just decided last Tuesday."

"Oh, good." Helen sighed and put John's cup away. "I'm glad they know we're going, and I'll write them a letter. We didn't know exactly where they were livin'."

"We got to talkin' and laughin' about all the times we watched the motion pictures they showed on the side of the feed store there in Upland," Bill said.

Throwing his head back John started to laugh. "And remember all those races we had in our cars, driving backwards to see who could go through town the slowest."

"You boys sure were silly," Helen giggled. George and Ella joined in the laughter. It felt good to laugh. Helen felt some of her heaviness start to lift.

"I don't know why you're all laughin'," Gesina stomped over to the group, arms crossed in front of her chest. "I don't want to sit here and do nothin'. It's so hot."

"I know it's hot, Gesina. Here, come out of the sun." Helen patted the ground beside her and John.

"John, can I go with you when you go back to get the stuff from the truck?" Gesina asked.

"Yes, and I'll just have to see if we can find a piece of candy for you in town."

"Oh, I would like a piece." Gesina gave John one of her rare smiles.

"Gesina, you don't need to go and you don't need candy," Mary said. She walked toward her and Gesina quickly crawled in between John and Helen.

"Ma, it's not going to hurt to let her come along and a little candy won't hurt her, either." John laughed at Gesina.

"You just spoil her." Mary wiped her face with her apron.

"George, do you want any candy?" John asked his younger brother.

"Sure."

Helen looked at Ella and smiled. "Ella and I would like some, too."

"Okay, okay, I'll get some for everyone."

That night, while Mary and the girls fixed dinner, the men set up the tent. Harmon, Mary and Gesina slept in the tent on the mattresses they'd brought. George slept in the truck.

John and Helen and Bill and Ella laid the thin cotton mattresses on the cement floor under the roof of the abandoned filling station. Later in the night it started to thunder and lighting and the rain came. The two young couples first slept on one side of the filling station and the rain blew in on them. Then they moved to the other side, and the rain drenched them there. They didn't get much sleep that night, with all the moving back and forth.

"I can't believe this, it rains here just when we're leaving," George yelled. He stuck his head out the window of the truck and felt the cool rain on his face. They all laughed with him.

They picked up the truck the next day about noon. They rearranged the load and put Helen's and John's trunk and mattress into the truck. They put the tent, camp stove, table, and food next to the tailgate. Once again they started west. John led the way, Bill drove the truck, and Ella followed. They traveled the new road, Highway 30, until it ran out. The government was still building the road, part of the Lincoln Highway that would eventually run from New York City to San Francisco. They were eight miles west of Lexington when the road cut back over to the old Highway 30 and they headed toward Cozad. They drove past the farm where Helen lived as a child and past the farm her grandparents had once owned. Just before they arrived in Cozad they passed the cemetery where Helen's father was buried. She waved as they went by. "*I love you, Dad,*" she whispered into the air.

Just east of Cozad a back tire went flat on the truck. They stopped in a field and set up camp while Bill and John took the tire into town to get it repaired.

"We sure haven't had good luck so far on this trip - first the truck needs to be fixed and then the tire on the truck goes flat." Bill sipped his second cup of coffee. Supper was finished and the women were washing up.

"Do you think this will keep on happening?" Ella asked. She handed the dish she had just washed to Helen to be dried. "Bill, we don't have much money and we need to get to Oregon as soon as possible."

"Helen and I also need to be careful with our cash," John said. "But we don't have much control over events. We'll just have to deal with what comes up. None of us has anything to go back to, so we need to keep moving west."

"Right!" Bill nodded his head. "Things have to be better in Oregon."

"I hope so." Ella dumped the dishwater and wiped her hands on her apron.

"Dora wouldn't have said to come if there wasn't work." Mary fanned her face with her apron. "It sure is hot. I'm glad we found this campsite."

"Bill," John turned to his brother. "We need to have a plan for dealing with problems and decide who will make a final decision."

"Well, goin' to Oregon was my idea, so it should be me."

"I don't agree. I think we should make a decision as a group. We're all traveling on this trip. So I think we need to take a vote on big issues."

"That sounds fair." Ella sat down beside Bill. "Don't you agree, Bill?"

"I guess. Ma, what do you think?"

"Everyone should have a say," Mary agreed.

"All right." Bill rubbed his chin. "But John, what about decisions that involve you and me? How do we handle those?"

John winked at Helen. "We can flip a coin."

Bill laughed. "Okay."

After supper and after things were cleaned up and put away, John and Helen drove into town to visit with her Uncle Tom. He owned the Hamburger Hut, and it was still open when they arrived.

"Well, hello Helen and John! What are you two doing in town?" Tom asked. He stood behind the grill and flipped hamburgers and pulled french fries out of the hot grease. "Just a sec, I have this order to fill." After serving his customers, he sat down on the stool beside Helen.

"Girl, how are you?"

"Fine, Uncle Tom. Johnny and I and his family are headed for Oregon."

"The truck had a flat tire and we're camped out of town for the night." John shook Tom's hand.

"No kidding, I plan to go there sometime soon myself. I have some brochures about Oregon. Would you like to see them?" Tom reached behind the counter for them.

"Yes." Helen started to read.

"How about a burger? I can fix one up fast, my treat." Tom moved behind the counter.

Helen and John looked at each other and grinned. "Okay with us," John said.

"Johnny, listen to what this brochure says. It's called *Oregon Beckons with Opportunities.*"

Helen tucked her hair behind her ear and started reading aloud. "The average rainfall in Western Oregon is 35 inches, and most of the rainfall comes in the fall and winter months. Summer temperatures average about 65 degrees, winter 40.8 degrees. The valley soils of Western Oregon are deep, fertile and well suited to diversified farming. More than forty crops of commercial importance produce in abundance and highest perfection in this section. Crop failures are unknown. The lands of Oregon offer opportunity for men of limited capital as well as those of means." She glanced at John, "That means we could buy land, doesn't it?"

"Sure sounds like it," John said. He looked over her shoulder at the brochure. "I also like that part about no crop failures."

Helen nodded her head. "Look at all these pictures of pigs, cows, sheep, wheat and look at this picture of the trees - they are so tall and close together. And there's the Pacific Ocean. There sure is a lot of sand. It says they have fog on the ocean and along the Willamette River."

"Dora lives outside of Salem, and that's by the Willamette River, isn't it?" John asked.

"Yes, that's what it says."

Tom placed the hamburgers in front of them. "Wouldn't it be exciting to see the Pacific Ocean?" He gazed out the window.

"I'm really nervous of the earthquakes they have there. They frighten me," Helen said.

Tom laughed. "Helen, you survive tornadoes all the time. You'll be able to survive an earthquake, if it happens."

"I guess you're right." She took a big bite of her hamburger and sighed with pleasure. "This sure is good. Thanks, Uncle Tom."

AUGUST 13, 1934

She's running through the forest, trying to find her way back to camp. She can't see or hear anyone. The large trees drip with rain. It's dark and the trees are surrounded by brush. The brush scratches her as she tries to climb through. She calls and calls for Johnny, but he is nowhere around. She starts to cry, her tears making it harder to see. All of a sudden she walks out of the trees and onto sand. Before her is the Pacific Ocean. It is cold and gray, unwelcoming. The rain mixes with her tears and she appears to be in a fog. In the distance she sees Johnny, walking with his folks, but they are walking faster and faster away from her disappearing into the mist. She yells to them, but no sound comes out. She tries to run, but her feet are heavy and hard to lift from the sand. She falls sobbing to the ground, then lifts her head to the rain.

The sun peeks from behind a cloud and warms her. The cold and dampness start to spiral away. She can see Johnny in the distance, coming toward her and calling her name. As she stands to wave to him, the earth below her starts to shake. She tries to run to him, but the earth shakes harder and harder. A crack in the ground opens before her, separating them. The crack snakes across the ground getting wider.

"No! No!" She screams and wipes the tears from her face. As the earth continues to shake, she hears a soft whisper coming from a long distance... *Helen.... Helen.* She struggles to see who is calling her.

"Helen, Helen," John whispered as he shook her and snuggled his mouth into her neck. "Are you awake? You need to get up and help Ma get breakfast."

Helen turned toward John, awake on the mattress beside her. During the night they pulled the sheet up around their chins to ward off the cooler air. John kissed her and whispered her name.

Helen looked at him and felt the love that radiated from him. Her heart beat faster and her inner core started to gather heat.

"Good morning," she whispered. She encased his body in her arms and hugged him hard. "I had a bad dream about Oregon. Look, I'm still shaking."

"It's okay, Helen. Things will be fine. Just wait, you'll see."

"I know, but it'll be strange to see the ocean and the forests. It won't be flat with the grass waving in the wind." She sat up, shook out her dress, and pulled it over her head. She quickly combed her hair and slipped on her shoes. John gave her a playful spank as she bent over. She giggled.

"Shush, quiet." John's light blue eyes laughed at her. He put his finger to his lips and pointed to the nearby mattress where Bill and Ella were starting to wake.

"See you in a few minutes." Helen walked back beyond the old tree branch to relieve herself.

Dawn was just beginning to break when Helen made her way to the back of the truck where the two-burner kerosene stove was set up.

"Helen, you're finally up," Mary said. "I'll cook the pancakes. Are there enough eggs?"

"Yes, we have a dozen, but we'll need more for tomorrow."

"I'll get some when we stop in a town today." John poured coffee from the big pot that was on the second burner. "Boy, this coffee smells good." He handed a mugful to Helen as he moved the pot from the stove to the table.

Helen sipped her coffee and set a second cast iron skillet on the stove. She added lard and began to scramble the eggs. Ella poured coffee for the rest of the group. Harmon blew on his coffee to cool it and George rubbed the sleep from his eyes before he took his first sip. Ella handed a cup to Gesina, who sat on the ground, gazing off into the distance.

George stretched. "Boy, I miss havin' cream for coffee. Hope we find some along the way today."

"It's so hot it's hard to keep the cream from turnin'. We'd best get only a pint or so," Ella said, setting out tin plates and forks. The pancakes started bubbling and Mary flipped the first two. They were golden brown and the smell wafted through the air around the group. Everyone gathered around and stood waiting for breakfast. They laughed when George's stomach growled. Mary dished up pancakes and Helen parceled out the eggs. Silence fell over the group as they all ate.

"By the time we get the tent broken down and on the truck and the food cleaned up it'll be close to seven." John looked at the sky. "Looks like it's goin' be hot again today."

"Yeah. Ma, I'll put the box with lunch things at the back of the truck. Anything else?" Bill asked.

"Just the usual." Mary helped Ella and Helen pack up the skillets, coffee pot, plates and forks that had been washed with the water that had heated up while everyone ate breakfast.

"How is the flour holding out?" John asked.

"We ain't started on the second bag yet, so we're good for a bit," Mary said.

It was John's turn to drive the truck and George and Harmon joined him. Mary and Gesina rode with Helen. Bill and Ella lead the way in the Whippet. Tumbleweeds rolled in the fields and once in a while blew across the road in front of the car.

"Don't the tumbleweeds look like they're havin' fun? They look so carefree and go wherever the wind takes them, " Helen said.

Gesina laughed, and Helen could see her nodding in the rear view mirror.

"That's silly thinkin'." Mary shook her head. "What a notion."

Helen just winked at Gesina and Gesina smiled back, her hand over her mouth.

Midmorning the caravan stopped at a small grocery store in Hershey. "I sure hope they've got some maple bars or warm cinnamon rolls," John said. Everyone laughed because John had to feed his sweet tooth. He came out of the store with enough cinnamon rolls for everyone and the warm sugary smell made everyone hungry. "I got a dozen eggs and some canned sardines for lunch. Bread is thirty-seven cents, about the same as at home."

From the time they left Kearney the highway had gradually climbed in elevation. Like at home, the fields were dry and cracked with withered wheat and corn stalks. Dirt-choked air swirled everywhere. Ahead of them they could see an outline of the mountains, but on either side of the road the prairies went on forever.

For the noon rest, they stopped under a shaded area just off the road near Big Springs, Nebraska. They splashed water on their faces and the shade helped everyone cool down a little. It was 100 degrees in the sun.

"George, set up the table under the tree," Mary commanded.

"It's a good thing you brought all this baked bread, Mom Schafer," Helen said, slicing the bread for sandwiches. "It's good. Who wants lunchmeat and who wants sardines? I'm also opening another jar of dill pickles and we still have watermelon."

"I'm selling water or cold coffee," Ella said as she handed out tin cups. The coffee was left over from breakfast. Glass bottles held the water and George and Gesina would fill them when water was available. The bottles were covered in gunnysack then wrapped with leather strips. The gunnysack was soaked in water and hung from the truck so the movement of the bottle would keep the water cool.

They rested in the shade for about an hour.

"Time to go," John called.

"I'm too tired to travel anymore today," Gesina pouted.

"Get into the car and hush up!" her mother yelled.

Just after the noon stop they started the steep climb that would take them into the mountains. They had to shift down into first gear. Helen was driving and had a hard time getting the clutch and gearshift to work together. There were large rocks lying by the road and a dry creek bed ran along it. In the middle of the afternoon they stopped for a rest and shared the remaining cinnamon rolls. They drank water every chance they got. Helen stood at the edge of the road, shaded her eyes and looked down onto the prairie. She could see for miles.

John walked up and put his arm around her. "Homesick?" he asked.

Helen shook her head. "No, not that. I used to read books about how the Indians were able to see a wagon train coming for days, and I couldn't figure out how. But standing here looking down, I think we could see a wagon train from a long ways away, couldn't we?"

"Well, we'd sure be able to see the dust it kicked up." John wiped his head with his handkerchief and put his straw hat on his head. "Best get started again."

Towards evening, John slowed the truck, stuck his head out the window and pointed to a spot near an embankment. "Think that'll work for tonight?" He hollered at Bill over the noise of the vehicles.

"Yeah, that looks good, and it's almost seven o'clock. Let's set up camp here."

"George, go see if you can find water anywhere near," John said after he had parked the truck. He turned to Bill. "We went about two hundred ten miles today."

"Yeah, felt good to get some highway under us, didn't it?" Bill removed his hat and wiped his head with his handkerchief.

"Someone get the stove set up and I'll get dinner cookin'," Mary said. "Helen and Ella, get some potatoes and an onion peeled while I get this canned meat heated up. Do y'all want canned corn or green beans tonight?"

"Corn," Harmon muttered.

"Gesina, open up a jar of corn and one of tomatoes," Mary said. "Fast, Gesina, fast."

Gesina jumped up, ran and got a jar of corn and one of tomatoes and brought them to the stove. "Here Ma, I opened them and the corn's ready to put in the pan."

"John, there's water right over there," George said, pointing north. "It's a good thing we stopped for cream in the last town; I can hardly wait for coffee tonight." He lifted the table from the truck and set it on the ground.

"Yeah, we had to buy a quart, but we can always have some of Ma's bread and cream for dessert tonight. We still have sugar don't we?" John asked.

"Plenty of sugar," Ella called.

Once again they lined up for food, getting ready for fried potatoes, corn and beef from the stove and spooning the tomatoes right from the jar. After the evening chores were finished, Helen got her paper and pen from the suitcase. "Who you gonna write to?" John asked. He laid on the ground with his head in her lap.

Helen smiled at him. "To Mom and Dick. I want to let them know how things are going. I won't be long."

August 13, 1934

Dear Mom and Dick,

I miss you both, but we're seeing a lot of new country. We've stopped for the night just east of Cheyenne, Wyoming. Supper is done and there's still enough light for me to write this letter. I'll mail it in one of the towns we go through tomorrow.

The mountains are so different from the grass plains of Nebraska. As we climbed the mountains there were rocks and huge boulders everywhere. It is still hot during the day and the winds blow here constantly. It does cool off a little at night. The ground almost looks black at times and is really dried out, not many plants around. We can see the mountain peaks, but they don't have snow and look dry. We are camped tonight along a big dirt embankment next to a railroad track. There are a few scrawny trees around. We stopped here because we only have to walk a bit north to get water to fill our jugs. There is a water tank for cattle and the guys said they probably load cattle onto the train here. It's dusty and the dirt from the embankment blows around when the wind gusts. There isn't anyplace around with green grass or shade.

We've had trouble with the truck and haven't been making good time, but we did go two hundred miles today. The Rocky Mountains just seem to get higher and higher. Gesina is frightened; she's heard those old stories about falling off the mountains. The only mountains she's seen are in her geography book at school. She's homesick. The farthest away from home she's been is forty miles when she came to stay with Johnny and me in Kearney.

We've fallen into a travel routine. Johnny leads the way in our car, Bill follows in the truck, and Ella brings up the rear. When Johnny drives the truck, Bill leads the way and I follow in our car. It's scary driving up these mountains, but we make it fine. Johnny is unhappy that he didn't bring the trailer. We could have brought all our things, but he listened to people who said you couldn't pull a trailer over the Rockies.

We get up with the first morning light, have breakfast and then have a cold lunch around noon. We stop in the evening around 6:30 or 7:00 pm when we find a good place and have a hot supper using the camp stove. Mary is in charge of the meals, so Ella and I do what she tells us. We had canned beef and the usual fried potatoes tonight, so Ella and I peeled potatoes. The food isn't fancy, but does fill us up.

Mary, Dad Schafer and Gesina sleep in the tent. Bill and Ella and Johnny and I sleep on the ground nearby. Sure glad we brought our mattress. George either sleeps in one of the cars or the truck. Dad Schafer and George set up camp each night and then break it down in the morning.

Johnny and I stopped in Cozad to see Uncle Tom. He had some brochures about Oregon he let us read. Hope it is as beautiful as the brochures say.

Ella and I are becoming friends. I never really had a chance to visit with her before. We only talked briefly whenever we went to Johnny's folks' place. We're the ones "outside" the family, so we rely on each other. She makes me laugh and doesn't take things too seriously.

Johnny is taking good care of me. He makes sure on the days I drive the car that I don't have any trouble keeping up. Course, I have to drive a ways back 'cause of all the dust.

There isn't much traffic on the road and rarely is anyone headed east. Everyone's going west. We see a few homes here and there, most empty. It's pretty desolate except in towns. The drought hit here, also.

We picked up a free map of Wyoming when we stopped for gas today. Gas ranges from nineteen to twenty-one cents a gallon, so pretty much the same as in Kearney. The roads are graveled. They're doing a lot of roadwork and when we make a detour, which is often, we drive on dirt roads.

It's time for bed and I'm tired so will close for now. Morning comes early. I will write again soon.

Love, Helen

Bill and Ella's Wedding Photo – June 19, 1933

AUGUST 14, 1934

The next morning, the group struggled to get up. Several trains went by during the night, and no one got much sleep. There was simply no relief from the heat. Even in the early morning it was hot, and would be hotter by the end of the day.

They started out after breakfast and continued their climb up the Rockies. They had traveled about fifty-six miles when they saw the sign for the summit: 8,640 feet. Shortly thereafter they passed through Laramie, Wyoming. The road began to drop slightly in elevation and went north around Elk Mountain. They went through Bosler and Rock River, stopping for lunch at Medicine Bow.

They sat on the ground and ate while they kept watch on a rock formation that was on slightly higher ground. The rock rose from a broad base to a point where another oblong-shaped rock balanced on the point of the base. The top rock looked like it could fall at any moment.

"If that top rock fell off the point, do you think it would roll all the way down to us?" Helen chewed her sardine sandwich.

"Don't know." John took a sip of his coffee. "Maybe."

"It would make a large noise when it fell off, wouldn't it?" George squinted up at the rock.

"Probably," Ella replied.

The group sat in silent contemplation and kept their eyes on the rock

"I hope it doesn't fall," Gesina started to cry. "It would probably roll over here and kill us all. That's what happens when you go places that are different than home."

"Gesina, new experiences are good for us," Bill said. "It's exciting to see new country and different things."

"I just want to go home."

Helen put her arms around Gesina. "We need you with us. Otherwise we wouldn't be complete. Our family makes our home. What would we do without you?"

"I want to be with my family; I just want us all to be at home in Nebraska."

"Well that's not going to happen, so stop being so sad and unhappy," Bill snapped.

"I'll try," Gesina sniffled as she wiped her eyes with her handkerchief and ran her hands through her uncovered black hair. She swished the skirt of her print dress and retied the bow at the back of it. Standing a little straighter, she picked up her straw hat and put it on her head.

"Gesina, help clean up the food." Mary started to pack the food items. "How long before we start again?"

"Oh, about fifteen minutes," John said. "What do you think, Dad?"

"Yeah, that's good," Harmon mumbled. He struggled to rise from sitting on the ground.

The men went in one direction and the women in another to relieve themselves before they started the afternoon drive.

That afternoon, east of Rawlins, Wyoming, they passed the Continental Divide. They stopped for a drink of water. "What is the Continental Divide?" George read the sign along the side of the road.

"The Continental Divide is where water on the east runs downhill to the Mississippi and the water on the west runs downhill to the Pacific Ocean," Ella replied in her schoolteacher voice.

John and Bill looked at each other and grinned. One went to the west side of the road and the other went to the east side, and they each made a puddle, but the water just sat there. "Guess our river isn't large enough," John laughed. As they traveled west they could see a wagon high on the side of the mountain.

"What is that?" Helen pointed to the wagon when they stopped for the afternoon break. "It looks like a gypsy wagon."

"It does, doesn't it?" John said. "I'm not sure what it is. I'll ask next time we stop for gas."

It was late afternoon when a rear tire on the truck went flat. John and Bill put the tire in the Ford and once again backtracked to have it fixed.

Helen and Ella sat on the ground, the truck providing some shade in the sparse grass alongside the road. Harmon, Mary and George were resting in the Whippet. Gesina was taking a nap in the truck.

"It sure is hot." Helen lifted the hair off her neck.

"Yes, just like always, it still must be over one hundred degrees." Ella took a sip of water and handed the cup to Helen. "At the rate we're goin', it'll take us forever to get to Oregon."

"Johnny said we made about two hundred sixty six miles today so that's really good for us, the best we've done so far." Helen took a drink of water. "I'm a little more confident driving Johnny's car now. Shifting is getting easier, though the drive up the mountains was really scary. How're you doin'?"

"Considering the only driving I did before this trip was driving in and out of my dad's garage, I'm doin' okay. It's hard when Mary rides with me. She doesn't know how to drive, but she sure knows how to tell me what to do." Ella chuckled and moved a stick around in the dirt.

"She doesn't approve of me, calls me 'town girl', but she likes you because you taught school." Helen returned the cup to the nail by the water jugs.

"Don't worry about it, Helen." Ella gave her a hug. "She finds lots of things that I do wrong and brings each and every one to my attention, too."

The two were quiet for a moment, each caught up in their own thoughts.

"You know, I don't think I know how you met Bill, " Helen said. "You lived in Riverton, didn't you? How far is that from Upland?"

"It's about thirty miles south of Upland. Mary and Augusta, my sister, belonged to the same quilting group and the group had a house dance. The dance was at Augusta's place; she's married to Johnny Scharff. I think you've met him."

"Isn't Scharff your maiden name?" Helen scratched her head.

"Yes, Johnny Scharff is our second cousin."

"Oh. I didn't think second cousins were supposed to get married."

"Well that didn't stop Augusta and Johnny, and they seem happy. Anyway, Bill drove his parents to the dance and stayed for the evening. Bill asked me to dance with him." Ella remembered how excited she was when he asked her to dance. He was such a tall, handsome man. "He was a terrible dancer, but I liked him. He invited me out the next Saturday night. Then when I told my best friend about Bill, she told me he had also invited her out the same Saturday night. We just had to wait and see what would happen."

"Goodness, what did happen?" Helen asked, eyes wide.

Ella blushed. "Well, Bill showed up on Saturday night with another man for my best friend and I went with Bill."

"How long did you go together before you got married?"

"Thirteen months, although we did break up once. There was someone who I was interested in, but I finally decided I really loved Bill."

Ella's eyes got a faraway look in them. She shook her head and continued. "I've even taught Bill how to dance and he is really good at it now."

"I know, I've danced with him and he's good." Helen fanned herself with her straw hat. "Didn't you elope? What was your wedding like?"

Ella nodded as she remembered June 19, 1933, their wedding day. "We drove to Smith Center Kansas, which is just across the state line and got a license at the courthouse. Then we went to the Methodist Church and were married by Reverend Jelkin. The Reverend's wife stood up for us."

"Why'd you elope?"

"Well, for two reasons really." Ella idly wrote her and Bill's names in the dirt. "First, my folks didn't want me to marry Bill. They called him a dirt farmer, and wouldn't give their blessing, so we decided to get married anyway and not tell them."

"Did you tell anyone?" Helen leaned forward to hear Ella's soft voice.

"Yes, Bill's folks knew about the wedding, but it was seven weeks before anyone else found out."

"Were your folks mad?"

"Dad came out carrying his shotgun and told Bill to get off his property. He said he would have the marriage annulled, but we both told him that we would just get married again. He finally accepted the marriage, but he wasn't happy."

"Oh my, that must have been scary," Helen gasped. Her eyes widened at the thought of such a confrontation. "What was the other reason you eloped?"

"During high school I'd taken normal training - that's general education but the last two years included teacher training. Then the summer after I graduated I took some additional teaching classes. I passed the test and got a three-year teaching certificate. In September '32 I taught in a one-room cabin south of Riverton, and I signed the contract that stated if I got married I would have to quit. They don't allow married women to teach school."

"So you were secretly married the whole second year you taught school?"

"Yes, the first year I had five pupils and made forty dollars a month but paid twelve dollars room and board and lived with my aunt and uncle. The second year I still made forty dollars a month but had to pay fourteen dollars room and board. I made twenty-six dollars a month, still good wages. Bill was working in Upland and he picked me up every Friday after school and then brought me back Sunday evening."

"I wish I could have graduated from high school," Helen sighed. "I only had four months left, but of course you can't attend high school if you're married. Johnny wanted to rent Mom's farm and we needed to start planting by March 1st, so we got married on February 28th. Johnny only went through the eighth grade, but he can read and write and do figures good."

"Bill, too."

"Here comes Gesina." Ella shaded her eyes. "I hope she had a good nap."

"Hi, Gesina," Helen called to the young girl. "Are you hot, too?"

Gesina scowled as she stomped over to where the two women sat. "Yes, and I wish they'd get back with the tire. I'm tired of waiting for them."

"They'll be along soon." Ella patted the ground next to her for Gesina to sit down and join them. "Would you like a sip of water?"

When the men returned they decided to drive a ways before they made camp. They stopped in an empty field across the road from several brick houses. The houses were full of Negroes who were peeking out the windows. George and John had gotten water and had begun to set up camp when a man from the filling station about a mile up the hill drove into their campsite.

"You don't want to stay here tonight, you won't have nothin' left in the morning," he said. His eyes darted toward the brick houses. "I stay in my filling station all night; I don't sleep and I keep a gun there. You come up and stay behind the station and you'll be safe there." They packed everything up and followed him back.

Later that evening, Helen and John lay on the mattress behind the filling station gazing at the stars. "I asked in town and those wagons that look like gypsy wagons are sheepherder huts," John said. "A sheepherder takes sheep high in the mountains for the summer and takes along his covered wagon. He cooks in it and it also has a bed for when the weather is bad. His job is to protect the sheep from wolves and other predators."

"Thanks for asking for me." Helen smiled at him and leaned over and gave him a big kiss.

"Yum, that tastes good, how about some more of those?" John snuggled down beside her on the mattress. The stars twinkled bright above them and as Helen felt John's body next to hers, she knew that as long as she was with him, she was home. Even here behind a filling station…she was home.

The next morning, just west of Green River, Wyoming, the road split; Highway 30S continued all the way to San Francisco, and Highway 30N went to Oregon. They turned north.

They were traveling on a dirt road detour, going up a steep hill, when Bill tried to shift the truck into a lower gear, but the gear wouldn't engage. He stopped the truck.

"Dad," Bill kept his foot on the brake. "Find something to put behind the wheel."

Harmon got out of the truck and found a couple big rocks and put them behind the two back wheels to keep the truck from rolling backwards. Bill turned the motor off and he and John scooted under the car to see why the gear wouldn't engage. Everyone gathered around the truck and talked quietly.

"Look here," John said. "It looks like we've lost the pin for first gear."

"Yeah. What do you think we can use to fix it?"

"I think we have some nails in the back. Do you think a nail would hold it?"

"We'll have to give it a try." They crawled from beneath the truck.

"George, can you get into the truck and find the sack of nails for us?" John asked. He brushed the dirt off his overalls.

George scrambled into the truck bed and after a few moments called out, "I found 'em; which size do you want?"

"Bring 'em all; we'll have to try 'em to find the right size."

With their heads together, John and Bill discussed what the best solution might be. To determine who would crawl under the truck John reached into his pocket and flipped a coin. John got into the cab and Bill went under the truck with the sack of nails.

"Okay," Bill called. "Shift down into first gear and hold your foot on the brake."

Ella was wringing her hands. "Bill, be careful."

"I will," he replied.

John kept his foot on the brake while Bill tried several different nail sizes.

"Think I have one that will work." Bill hammered the nail end over the gear so it would stay in place. Bill scrambled from under the truck. "Okay, John; give it a try."

John started the motor carefully, pressing his right foot down on the gas pedal while at the same time slowly easing his left foot off the clutch. The truck started to move and he drove to the top of the hill before he stopped. Everyone piled into the cars and quickly caught up with him.

They drove about sixty miles. In Diamondville, Wyoming, they stopped by a small stream where a few trees provided shade. While they washed up and drank coffee, John walked to the store and bought some maple bars.

They passed through Kremmer, Wyoming, where the first J.C. Penny store had been built in 1902, then stopped for an afternoon break at Soda Springs, Idaho, about fifty-eight miles beyond the Wyoming border.

"It sure smells here, doesn't it?" Helen held her nose. "Like rotten eggs."

"That's the sulfur," John said. "The health resort here has sulfur springs they use for healin'."

"It may smell, but it sure is beautiful," Ella said. "Look at how green the trees are and the cooler temperature feels so nice on my skin." She took off her shoes and socks and buried her feet in the tall grass.

Gesina was lying on the grass with her eyes closed, a slight smile on her face. "It does feel nice here, but I'm getting a headache."

They walked to look at the sulfur pool. "It sure would feel good to get washed off. None of us have had a bath since we left home," Mary said.

"Yeah, we'd probably smell better, too, but none of us has a bathing suit," Bill said, looking at the blue water in the pool. "It looks inviting, but it smells bad."

That night they camped along the Snake River before American Falls Reservoir, about twenty-six miles west of Pocatello. They arrived fairly late that night, but in the distance they could see a big building beside the lake. It was surrounded by sand. It was beautiful there, and cooler than it had been. The mosquitoes were so thick that Harmon had to light cattails soaked in kerosene to keep them away.

"Do you think we could go into the river here to wash up?" George asked. He scratched his leg.

"I'm not sure how deep it is here; better not," Harmon said. "None of ya know how to swim."

After supper was cleaned up, Helen yawned and stood up and brushed off her skirt. "The water on the stove should be warm by now. I'm gonna wash up."

"Let me hold the blanket up for you, then you can hold it for me," Ella said. "Let's help each other wash our hair. Gesina, do you want to wash tonight?"

"No. I'm tired; I'm goin' to bed."

The next morning George got up early and started walking toward the building next to the lake.

"Where are you going?" his father asked as he stuck his head out of the tent.

"I'm goin' to walk over to see what that is." George pointed to the tower.

"I'll walk with you," Harmon said, reaching back into the tent for his hat.

The young man stood straight and tall while Harmon was bent over at the shoulders and walked with a slight shuffle. Their silence was comfortable.

At the base of the tower, they looked in and decided to walk up the stairs. The old wooden stairs spiraled up. After a few times around the stairs, Harmon stopped and wiped his head with his handkerchief. "I'm not goin' to go up; I'm getting dizzy and I might fall off. You go ahead, but be careful."

George climbed to the top and saw two tanks inside the tower, and from the top he could see the whole lake. He looked down on their campsite and saw his mother starting to make breakfast. On the way back to camp, Harmon and George talked with a man walking his dog on the beach.

"Why is there a lighthouse on the lake?" George asked.

"Years ago the place that ground grain was across the lake at American Falls. It took too long for a team of horses to go around the lake, so they went across the lake with boats. It took nine hours to cross the lake and then it took one day to grind the wheat and another nine hours to get back. The lighthouse was to help the boats find their way back as it was usually dark by the time they returned. When the railroad came through, they no longer used boats and the lighthouse was never used again."

"What are the tanks inside the building for?" George asked.

"One is a carbide tank and the other one holds water. When water is dripped onto the carbide, it generates a gas to light the lamp at the top of the lighthouse."

* * * * *

They'd gone four miles that morning when the truck had another flat tire. Everyone waited at American Falls while John and Bill drove back to Pocatello to get the tire fixed.

While they waited, Harmon, Mary and George sat under the shade of some trees and drank cold coffee. Helen and Ella sat together and watched the falls while Gesina lay on the ground beside them.

"It looks so refreshing doesn't it?" Ella smiled.

"Yes, and it's even cooler than yesterday. It sure is pretty around here, although things look dry."

"Gesina, sit up! Why are you lying on the ground?" Mary stomped over to where Gesina had stretched out.

"I don't feel good, Ma." Gesina started to cry.

"Just never mind, you're fine," Mary said. "Stop cryin' now."

"I think she might be running a fever," Helen said, putting her hand on Gesina's forehead. "She feels hot."

"I'll get a cloth for her forehead." Ella jumped up and got a dishcloth and wet it with water from the jugs hanging on the truck.

"That feels better, thanks," Gesina whispered. She closed her eyes and dropped off to sleep.

It was a couple hours later when the men returned and put the patched tire on the truck. About one hundred miles down the road, in Twin Falls, they saw a garage.

"Let's get the pin on the truck fixed and get the tires checked while we're here," Bill suggested.

That was the first time they had stopped at a garage with the truck. They had always just taken the tire or inner tube with them to be fixed.

"These tires don't fit and are being cut by the rims, that's why they are always going flat. I'll make you a good deal on a couple tires that will fit your rims," the garage attendant said.

"Okay, go ahead and put them on," John said. "Dad, you have some money to pay for the tires?"

* * * * *

As they approached Thousand Springs Falls, about forty miles west of Twin Falls, the road they were traveling made a steep drop into a valley. The incline was a nine or ten percent grade for about two miles. John and Bill stopped the vehicles and looked down the grade. "That's pretty steep," Bill said. "I think I should drive our car down. Ella isn't used to this steep of an incline."

"Neither is Helen," John said. He reached into his pocket for a coin. Bill called "heads."

John laughed and walked over to Helen. "I'm drivin' the truck down, and you'll have to drive the car."

"Down this hill? What if I go off the edge?"

"You'll do fine."

Helen took a deep breath. "I'll give it a try."

"If you have trouble, Bill will drive me back up to get you," John said as he got into the truck.

Helen waited at the top until the truck got to the bottom. She could see John standing beside the truck, waving her down. Helen looked down into the valley below and it looked like a checkerboard. From the crest where she was sitting in the car she could see fields everywhere. She was scared.

"Oh my," she said. "That's a long ways down."

Mary was with her. For once she didn't say a word. Helen shifted into first gear and slowly started down the hill, keeping her foot on the brake. Her hands were sweaty and the steering wheel kept slipping. She hugged the hillside, using the left lane. The right lane ran along the outside of the hill and the shoulder dropped off steeply into the valley. *"I'm glad no one's coming up the hill,"* she muttered to herself.

She was shaking when she got to the bottom and stopped the car beside the truck. She got out of the door and took a deep breath.

"Helen, you done good." John ran up and gave her a hug.

They stopped by the river that ran alongside the ravine and were able to wade in the water and rinse off their faces and arms. They felt refreshed.

The climb out of the valley was gradual.

They drove almost to Boise that night and made camp in a nice park. A man came over to Harmon and *bummed* him for money. "I don't have any money," Harmon said. "Do you want some bread and sardines?" The man left after Mary gave him a can of sardines and a loaf of bread. "We can't stay here tonight," Harmon told the group. "He'll be back and steal everything he can."

They couldn't risk losing the little they owned so they packed every-thing back on the truck and drove another ten miles, finally stopping beside a filling station where other people were camped. They felt safer with other travelers around.

That night as they were finishing up dinner a truck pulled into the filling station and parked next to their camp. A tired-looking woman started setting up camp while a man and four small children gathered wood and started a fire.

"Where you all headed?" the man called.

"We're goin' to Oregon," John said.

"Well, we had no luck in Oregon; couldn't get crops goin'. Rains all the time and the sun don't shine much. We're headed back home. Hope you all have better luck than us."

"Where did you farm?" John and Bill walked to the fire and squatted to watch the man build the fire.

"In the hills outside Corvallis, in the coast range."

"We're headin' to Pratum, in the Willamette Valley. We have family there. They're doin' okay and say they have work for us."

"Well, good luck to you." The man settled the black coffee pot in the middle of the fire.

That night as they lay on their mattress and looked at the stars, Helen turned to John. "What if we can't make any money when we get to Oregon? What will we do?"

"Don't worry, Helen. Did you see that man's truck? It was all rusted out and just holding together. Looks like he doesn't take care of his things. He probably didn't have the tools he needed to earn a living. Things are different with us. We're young. We don't have any kids, and we can both work hard. We'll be fine." John brushed Helen's hair out of her eyes, pulling her into his arms.

Wiping the tears from her eyes, Helen whispered, "Are you sure?"

"Dora and Mick will help us out 'til we get on our feet, you'll see. That's the advantage of goin' to family."

Balancing his breakfast plate on his knees, Bill sat next to his wife. "That man camping next to us last night didn't have good luck farming in Oregon."

"No, he sure didn't. The soil around here really looks good, nice and dark and silky looking." Ella took a bite of her second pancake. "There're crops right alongside the road and we've gotten fresh corn and tomatoes off the food stands. We could probably find work here in the fields."

"Yeah, but Dora is expecting us," Bill said. "I told 'em we're coming."

"I'm for goin' anywhere we can make money," George said as he stood by the stove waiting for his pancakes.

"It's green here, and a lot cooler than home, but I think we should go on to Dora's. If we can't find work, we can always come back." John filled his coffee cup for the second time. "We're only about three hundred fifty miles or so from Pratum."

Ella brushed her hair out of her eyes. "But we only have about twenty dollars left. Maybe we should stop a day or two and earn some money."

"I know, I know." Bill looked at his older brother. "John, what do you think about stopping and working a couple of days?"

John was silent for a moment. "You and Ella can stay and work if you want. Then you can come when you have more money."

Helen just listened. She was going wherever Johnny went.

Bill turned and looked at his mother. "Ma, what do you think?"

"I'm goin' to Dora's. We need to be close to family." Mary used her apron as a hot pad and moved the skillet off the cook stove. "We started together, and we need to stay together."

"Dad, what about you?"

Harmon nodded his dark head. "To Oregon. That's where I told Henry we was goin'."

"Well, I guess we should stay with the family." Bill looked at Ella.

"Okay." Ella sighed and nodded her head.

"Dad or I will help out if you run short of cash," John said, tossing the last of his coffee onto the ground. "Okay, Oregon it is. Let's get this show on the road."

Gesina was still fighting a headache and wasn't hungry. She rode in the back seat of the car with John and Helen. George carried his rolled up pancakes into the truck cab to ride with Harmon and Bill. Ella and Mary brought up the rear. As Ella and Mary drove by a house that was standing empty, a man without any pants jumped into an open doorway and lifted his shirt to expose himself. Ella was so surprised she slammed on the brakes and brought the car to a screeching stop. Mary's mouth hung open as she stared at the man.

"Oh, my." Ella stomped on the gas. "We'd better get out of here." Mary and Ella looked at each other and laughed. They'd have fun telling their story at lunch.

"Look, Dad," George said, pointing out the truck window at the sign that said 'Welcome to Oregon.' "We're in Oregon."

"Finally!" Bill shouted, tooting the horn.

Harmon nodded and grinned.

They stopped for gas at a filling station near Meacham. Ella, remembering all the times Bill told her not to park so far behind him, pulled in right behind the truck. They all filled up and as they were leaving Bill backed up the truck right into the Whippet and crushed the radiator.

"Ella, why did you park right behind me?" Bill walked around the car and kicked the tires with his foot.

"Bill, you keep telling me to pull right in behind you, and that's what I did." Tears started to gather in Ella's eyes. "I'm sorry."

"It's no one's fault, just the way our luck has been runnin'." John came over and looked at the leaking radiator. "Let's see if they can fix it here at the fillin' station."

They were unable to get the radiator fixed and had to stop every few miles to add water to it. At Cabbage Hill they began the long downgrade into Pendleton. Bill drove the Whippet, John the truck and Helen once again had to make a steep descent driving the Ford. Bill coasted most of the way, but Helen drove in first gear. At least this time she was driving down on the side of the road closest to the hillside.

The road seemed to wind around and around the mountain. There was some traffic traveling up the mountain so she had to be careful to stay in her lane. Again, Helen was shaking when she reached the bottom of the steep hill.

They stopped in a field just east of Pendleton. While Bill took the car into town to get the radiator fixed, the rest of the group set up camp under a large oak tree. When Bill hadn't returned after a while, John drove into town to check on him. A hot wind blew through the wheat fields, but it was still cooler than it had been in Nebraska. The men were back within an hour. Slamming the car door shut, Bill strode over to the group. "They have to order a part for the radiator and it will be here sometime tomorrow. I guess we'll just stay here for a day or so."

"Bill, how much will it cost to get it fixed? Do we have enough money?" Ella picked at her skirt.

"We'll be able to manage, and John said he'd help out if we need it."

That evening after dinner everyone but Gesina took a spit bath, using a cloth to wash their bodies with soap and water and then rinsing the cloth out and using a clean pan of warm water to wash off the soap. They also helped one another wash their hair and the men shaved. John put on his clean pair of overalls and Helen put on her other dress. It was a blue print with a wide white collar and buttoned down the front.

"It sure feels good to get washed up a bit." John said

"You smell better, too." Helen laughed and snuggled up to him as they sat around the camp. For the third day, Gesina ran a temperature. To get her fever down, Mary sponged her off and let her sleep in the tent with the flaps open. They tried to give her water every time she woke up.

The next morning they slept in and had a leisurely day. Everyone enjoyed the break from travel. The men dusted down the inside of the vehicles and the women organized the remaining food items. Gesina was still lethargic and running a temperature. They spent a second night in the field.

August 18, 1934

Dear Mom and Dick,

I really miss you. I think of you all the time. Hopefully the heat wave will have broken for you. It's hot here, but cooler than at home. We're camped in a field just outside of Pendleton, Oregon. We're waiting to get Bill and Ella's Whippet fixed. Bill backed the truck into the car and broke the radiator. Thank goodness it wasn't me who did it.

We got here yesterday in the late afternoon and hopefully the car will be ready tomorrow morning. We've had a lot of truck problems that have really slowed us down. Mostly flat tires, but Harmon bought some tires that fit the rims on the truck a couple days ago and we haven't had a flat since.

Last night everyone took a spit bath and Johnny and I changed into our extra set of clothes. I hated to put the dirty clothes into the suitcase. I've shook out my dress every night, but it's still filthy. Johnny's overalls were so dirty, it felt like I was folding a board to get them to fit in the suitcase.

Gesina is ill and has run a temperature for the last few days. We're all concerned that she doesn't eat or drink anything. When we leave here Johnny will put a pillow down in the back seat of our car and she will ride there so she can stretch out. We'll keep the windows open so she can get whatever breeze there is.

We hope to get to Pratum within the next day or two; our funds are getting low and we need to make some money. Our food supply is holding out and gas has been pretty evenly priced. Johnny says gas is nineteen cents a gallon here in Pendleton.

There's a little more traffic going east now, but the majority still travels west with us. For the last few nights, a man traveling in an Austin Healey camps wherever we camp. He usually leaves about the same time as we do each morning, but he always comes in about an hour behind us. He's traveling from New York to Portland. He said it's safer staying near other people.

We've always felt safe, although we did change campsites one night when someone begged for money and Harmon thought we should move to a different place.

I hope you are both well. I miss you both so much.

Love, Helen

The next morning they ate a late breakfast and drove into town to pick up the Whippet. They were traveling again by 11 a.m. They stopped in Hermiston and bought a large watermelon. Outside of Boardman the road dropped down into a gorge and they drove along the Columbia River.

At Celilo they heard a roar and then saw a large cascade of water falling from one level of the river to another. Along the side of the falls they could see wooden structures that stuck out over the falls. Indians were standing on the structures using long-handled nets to catch fish. Native American women were drying and smoking the fish over a fire along the bank of the river.

"What a beautiful waterfall," Helen shouted into John's ear. "What kind of fish are they catching?" She shaded her eyes looking across the water and pointed to the men on the wooden structure.

"Not sure." John slowed the car to a crawl. "I'll ask at the next stop."

Looking across the river into Washington they could see large smooth rolling hills, but on the Oregon side all they saw were rock cliffs about 300 feet high. The wind created white caps on the river.

West of The Dalles, the road started climbing and rock guardrails ran alongside the road. A series of graceful switchbacks led up the hillside and ahead they could see the road running back and forth all the way to the top. They had to stop a couple of times to add water to the truck's steaming radiator.

At the top they pulled into a viewpoint and looked back down the way they had come. They could see the river winding down from the east. They had never seen such a magnificent river.

"Who wants watermelon?" Helen asked, cutting it into sections. Everyone but Gesina had a piece for an afternoon snack.

"This is good." Harmon said as he spit watermelon seeds along side the road.

"This here place is called the Rowena Viewpoint." Walking back from reading the information board, John reached for a piece of watermelon. He kissed Helen on her cheek.

"What is the name of the road we're on?" Helen ducked her head, feeling the heat rise in her face.

"This is the Columbia River Scenic Highway. That's Washington State on the other side of the river." George leaned against the truck and munched on his second piece of watermelon. He had the Oregon map spread out on the back of the truck bed.

Far above them they could see three or four large birds soaring.

"Are those eagles? They sure look like eagles." Bill shaded his eyes.

"Maybe." John nodded toward the cars. "Let's get goin'."

Just west of Mosier they once again started to climb and after a few miles they reached the Twin Tunnels. The tunnels were just wide enough for two vehicles to pass. There was an arched entryway made of rock, and inside the tunnel it was cool. Light drifted in through two viewing portals, but they couldn't stop as there were other cars following them. One tunnel ended and a second started immediately, curving slightly to the right. After they passed through both tunnels, the uphill grade became steeper and they pulled into a turnout to allow the other cars to pass. While the men added water to the truck radiator, the women walked to the stone wall that enclosed the turnout. Helen rested her elbows on top of the wall. "Doesn't this breeze feel good? And just look at that beautiful view of the river."

The women removed their hats to let the breeze whip through their hair. "Yes, it is beautiful. There are a lot more trees now and I like the way they shade the road." Ella held out her dress to catch the wind.

Mary stood with her eyes closed and felt the wind billow through her skirt. "I hope we get to Pratum soon. I'm tired of this travelin' and Gesina needs to be out of the sun and rest where it's quiet."

"Johnny thinks we'll get there tomorrow, if we don't have any more problems with the truck." John tooted the horn and the women walked back to the vehicles.

They drove into Hood River and from the downtown area they could see a huge mountain. "Is that Mt. Hood?" Helen pointed south through the windshield to the mountain that seemed to tower over everything.

"I don't know. Look on the map," John said.

"From the map I would say yes. Isn't it beautiful?" Helen turned to tell Gesina to look, but she was asleep.

They stopped west of Hood River that evening and camped on the grounds of the Columbia Gorge hotel. The beautiful two-story hotel was closed, but there were trees for shade and they set up camp on green grass. They could hear a waterfall and followed the small creek to where it dropped about two hundred feet into the Columbia River. The creek water looked clear, but they used a water faucet outside the hotel to fill their water jugs. They fixed supper using the tomatoes and corn they'd purchased at a fruit stand earlier in the afternoon. Gesina didn't eat anything and would only sip water. Railroad tracks ran along the Columbia River and they heard a train pass by.

John wrapped his arms around Helen as they settled on the mattress for the night. "I asked in town about those falls we saw on the river today and it's called Celilo Falls. The Indians are catching salmon and steelhead fish."

"Do they sell the fish?" Helen yawned and pulled the sheet up over her body.

"They catch them for their own use, but sometimes they barter fish in exchange for something they want. Maybe we'll come back someday and see if we can barter for a fish."

"Okay," Helen murmured as she drifted off to sleep.

They started out early the next morning and had only gone four miles when a fan belt broke on the truck. John and Bill returned to Hood River to get a new one.

The rest of the group waited in the shade of a towering fir tree just off the road. A truck loaded with empty apple boxes came down the road toward them, slowed and then crossed the road and pulled in behind them.

"Need any help?" a large man called as he got out of his truck.

George walked toward him. "We're okay. Two of our party went back to Hood River to get a fan belt for our truck. They should be back soon. Thanks for stopping."

"I noticed the Nebraska license plates on the truck and car. I'm from Nebraska, too, and just wondered what area y'all are from."

"We started in Upland and the whole family is traveling to the Willamette Valley."

"My family is from Macon, not far from Upland."

"What's the family name?" George asked.

"Varwig," the tall man replied.

"Varwig?" George asked, stunned. "Varwig is my Ma's family name."

"What's her name now?"

"It's Mary Schafer."

The man looked at George and was silent for a moment. Then he looked around the area. "Is she traveling with you?"

"Yeah. She and my Pa are under the tree over there." George pointed to where his parents rested in the shade.

"I think I might know her."

"Really? You might know my Ma?" George brushed his dark hair back over his forehead. "I'll get her." George ran over to where his parents sat. "Ma, a man stopped to see if we needed help. He said he might know you."

Mary pulled herself up from the ground, brushed fir needles from the back of her skirt and walked back to the truck with George. Harmon followed slowly behind them.

The man had his hat off and looked at her carefully. Then he began to laugh and walked toward her. "Mary, it *is* you."

Mary stood still and squinted her eyes as she studied the man coming toward her. "Paul? Paul." Mary started to cry. "It's been years since you left home, and no one knew if you were dead or alive."

George looked at his mother. He couldn't remember seeing her cry. "Who's Paul?" he asked.

"My brother." Mary took a handkerchief out of her pocket and dabbed at her eyes.

"Brother. You mean he's my uncle? Have I ever met him?" George circled around his mother.

"No. Paul left home when he was twenty-one and we never heard from him again. John and Bill were young boys when he left. Now, hush up."

Paul bent down and planted a kiss on Mary's cheek. Holding his hat in his hands he took a few steps back. "I've traveled all around and I'm doin' okay. How's the folks?"

"Paul," Mary said as her checks turned pink. She looked up to see her younger brother's face. "I can't believe it's you. Pa died in 1930 and Ma's living in Franklin. Everyone wondered where you had gone. I didn't know you were in Oregon. Did you know Dora and Mick live outside Salem?"

"I knew she lived in Oregon somewhere, but I ain't located her yet. Is that where you're headin'?"

"Yeah, she said there's work for all of us here in Oregon." Mary shaded her eyes with her hand. "Things are really bad at home. Drought, dust storms, and no crops. When John and Bill - you remember them, don't you, from when they were boys - decided to come to Oregon, Harmon and I joined 'em. This is George, our third son, and our daughter Gesina is asleep under the tree."

"Harmon, good to see ya again." The men shook hands.

Paul nodded as he shook George's hand.

Just then John and Bill drove up in the Ford Tudor. George ran to the car. "Do you know who stopped to see if we needed help? It's Ma's brother, Paul. Can you believe that?"

"Paul, why, I haven't seen you since I was a kid," John said as he shook Paul's hand. "How ya doin'?"

"Doin' okay. I help with the apple harvest here at Ray Nichelson's orchard. Another half mile and I'd have turned off to the orchard." Paul shook his head in disbelief. "Then I would have missed y'all. Ya lookin' for work? I work for the owner of the orchard here and he'll begin pickin' apples in about three weeks. We can always use help with the harvest. Do ya want to pick apples then?"

"Helen and I would." John turned to Bill. "What about you and Ella?"

"Yeah. That would be good. How long does the harvest last?" Bill asked.

"Three to four weeks with the pickin' and packin'. Why don't you and John come and meet the boss and see if he'll hire you?" Paul said. "You can follow me in your car."

"Pa," John called excitedly, "Bill and I are goin' with Paul to see if we can get hired to pick apples next month. We should be back in about thirty minutes. Can you and George get the belt back on the truck while we're gone? We want to get to Pratum tonight and it'll probably take us four or five hours to drive there."

Harmon nodded.

"We'll get it done," George said. "I watched how you took it off."

John walked to Helen and kissed her. "We'll be right back. Why don't you and Ella make sandwiches for everyone to eat while we're drivin'. Do you think you'd like pickin' apples?"

"Sounds good," Helen and Ella said in unison.

Paul stood before his sister and took her hand. "I hope Oregon is good to ya, I sure like livin' here. Where does Dora live?"

"Pratum, just outside Salem. I hope y'all come see us. Dora will know where we are."

"Maybe I will." Paul turned and walked back to his truck, slapping his hat back on his head.

Just as John started up the Ford Tudor to follow Paul, George jumped on the running board. "John, why did Paul leave home?"

"If I remember right he and his dad had a falling out. Paul didn't want to be a farmer and left. No one has heard from him in years. Now, go on and fix the truck. We'll be back soon."

* * * * *

The men returned with a promise of jobs for the following month and the family started out again. The caravan traveled down the narrow, twisty road toward Portland. As they headed west they saw scrub oak, maple and fir trees and the forest became thicker and covered more of the hillside.

Outside of Cascade Locks the trees provided a canopy over the road and ferns were everywhere, the air quiet and still. They crossed the bridge over Eagle Creek and a little further on they saw some construction on the river.

"What are they building?" Helen turned in her seat to get a better view out the window.

"Paul said they're building a dam across the river. It'll be called the Bonneville Dam and will provide electric power for this area." John stretched his neck to see around Helen.

"How do they get all the large equipment and building materials up here? This road is pretty narrow."

"Probably float 'em up the river on a barge."

They continued west and saw several waterfalls; John idled the car as they looked at Multnomah Falls and the stone lodge nearby.

"We'll come back when we have more time," John promised.

The road twisted and climbed up to the Vista House where they stopped and looked down on the Columbia.

"How beautiful! I've never seen anything like this gorge," Helen said.

She could see the river as it traveled from the east and moved on to the west. It was blue and black with white caps scattered here and there. Both sides of the river had steep rock cliffs and the forest grew up and over the top of the cliffs.

Walking into the building, they used the restrooms they found on the lower floor. They traveled on down the highway and passed through Corbett and crossed the Sandy River at the Stark Street Bridge. Driving through farmland, they took Stark Street into Portland and turned south to Salem on 82nd Avenue. They passed through Oregon City, Aurora, Canby and Woodburn on highway 99E. As they drove down the valley they could see mountains to the east and high rolling hills to the west.

They arrived in Salem in the afternoon and stopped on Market Street at a filling station to get gas. There were trees along the road and a large maple tree shaded the filling station. A slight breeze moved the warm air.

Bill and George asked a man who was standing beside a truck for directions to Pratum. The man took off his hat and pointed east. "Just follow the signs down Market Street and it'll take you to Pratum. Who're you looking for?" he asked.

"McDougal."

"I know him. Why are you looking for him?"

"His wife and our mom are sisters," Bill said.

The man looked at them for a moment. "You mean Dora is your aunt?" The men nodded.

"I'm Ted Kleen. Follow me and I'll take you to your uncle's place."

"Kleen is your name? That's my grandma's maiden name," Bill exclaimed.

"Yep. I'm related to your ma."

"Not again," George shouted as he ran to the car. "Ma! Ma! This man's name is Kleen and he says he's related to you!"

The three vehicles followed Ted's truck out Market Street, onto Sunnyview Road and then to Pratum. It was warm and the windows in the car were down. John and Helen stayed back a ways to avoid the thick dust the truck created from the gravel road.

"It's good to see only dust from the gravel road and not dirt blowing in the window like back home," John remarked. He ran his hand through his hair.

"Look at how green things are, even in August." Helen glanced at the grove of fir trees along the road. "What beautiful flowering shrubs, I'll have to ask Aunt Dora what they're called."

Ted finally pulled over to the side of the road and walked back to John and Helen's car. Bill pulled the truck in behind John, and Ella parked behind the truck. Ted leaned on the window of the car, pushed back his hat, and pointed to the road that turned right.

"Take the right turn here and follow the road about two miles. Dora and Mick's is the second place. Tell them the Kleen family will be over to visit after supper. See you then."

"Thanks for helping us find our way," John said, shaking Ted's hand.

The group arrived at the McDougal home late in the afternoon. John pulled in beside the garage and turned off the engine. Silence surrounded them and excitement sparkled in their eyes. After nine long days on the road, they had arrived. Helen gazed at the green grass and the huge maple tree shading the house and yard. Beautiful flowers surrounded the house, and she could identify roses and hydrangeas. The house sat to the left of the driveway and the detached garage was to the right. There was a hay wagon by the barn and a mower sitting beside the hen house; Helen heard the chickens clucking. Horses and cows grazed in the pasture.

"It's lovely," Helen whispered. "It's so green. Can you feel that breeze?"

"Yes, it's nice here." John opened the door just as Bill tooted the horn.

Mick's six-foot frame filled the barn door. He waved and hurried toward them. The screen door slammed as Dora came running, her apron flapping in the wind and her light brown hair flowing with the breeze. She looked much like her sister, but slightly taller. Behind her children of various ages flowed from the house.

"You're finally here! We were worried about you. How long were you on the road?" Dora ran up and hugged everyone.

Mary hugged her sister. "It's been a long, hot trip."

Everyone started talking at once, laughing and crying.

"Kids, come meet your Aunt Mary and Uncle Harmon and your cousins," Dora called. She wrapped her arms around her three children as she made introductions.

"Come on in. Come on in." Mick waved his arms as he welcomed everyone. As they walked across the yard, Ella and Helen stopped at a pear tree. Pears were lying on the ground and they asked if they could have some. "Of course," Dora said. They picked the pears off the ground and started to eat them.

"Pick 'em from the tree," Mick instructed. "The ones on the ground are bruised and too ripe."

"These from the ground look beautiful," Helen replied. "I don't see any bruises. Wouldn't everyone at home enjoy these pears?" Ella nodded in agreement, the pear juice running down her arms. The men sampled the fruit, too. Harmon and Mary were still standing by the car when Mick turned to them.

"Where's Gesina?"

"Here in the car." Mary turned to the Ford. "She's been sick for the last three or four days and is running a fever. I'm worried about her."

"Here, let me take her." Mick reached into the car for Gesina. He lifted the thin girl into his arms and strode toward the house.

"She doesn't weigh anything. I'll find a cool place for her." He took her into one of the bedrooms on the main floor and sat her on the bed. He brought cool water, washed her face and hands, and gave her something to drink. "You just lie here and sleep now. You're home and everything will be fine. Rest now. We'll call you for supper." He pulled the window shade all the way down, and covered her with a handmade quilt. Gesina was finally able to lie still without feeling the movement of the car. She pulled the quilt up around her and cuddled into the soft mattress. Sleep moved over her gently.

Everyone trooped through the front door and dining room into the kitchen. On the left wall was a large black wood stove with a wood box beside it. Next to the back door a window, framed by flowered curtains, overlooked the back porch and yard. Below the window was a sink with a hand pump. The hutch and a worktable were across from the stove. On the round kitchen table was a tall vase filled with red roses.

Everyone lined up at the sink for a glass of cool water.

"I bet everyone is tired and hungry," Dora remarked. "I'll start supper. Why don't you girls freshen up in our bedroom and the guys can wash up at the bench on the back porch. The outhouse is behind the willow tree."

"Sounds wonderful," Helen sighed. "We have food we can contribute to supper."

"Let's not worry about that today; you just get washed up."

The women took spit baths and shook the road dust out of their dresses.

"Boy, this feels good doesn't it?" Ella commented. "To have arrived and to be washed up."

"Yes, it does." Helen fluffed her dark hair as she viewed herself in the mirror.

"Girls, stop fooling around and get out there and help Dora with the food," Mary chided.

Dora looked up from cutting the homemade bread. "We'll eat outside tonight. The men are setting up some boards for a table and they'll move the chairs out. Helen, can you stir these fried potatoes and put them in the blue dish? Ella, why don't you put the corn on that platter there on the hutch? And Mary, would you put these tablecloths on and set out the silverware?"

"Everything smells so good." Helen stirred the potatoes and onions. "Is everything from your garden?"

"Yes; we've had a dry year, not as much rain as usual. Actually the last two years have been drier than usual. Everything came on early, but the garden just keeps on producing. The kids use a bucket and ladle to water it every morning and evening."

John stuck his head in the back door. "Things smell wonderful in here. I'm getting hungry. I wanted to let the girls know that the thermometer on the back porch says it is eighty-eight degrees. It sure doesn't feel that warm."

"We often get a breeze in the late afternoon and evening that helps cool things down. At night the temperature usually drops into the fifties or so, not like back in Nebraska where it stays hot all night." Dora stopped talking for a moment as she dished up the fried chicken. "John, why don't you take this chicken out to the table? I cooked it this morning, hoping you would arrive in time for supper. I kept it cool in the cellar. We have milk, water and coffee to drink." Dora handed the platter of chicken to John and wiped her hands on her apron. "I think everything's ready. It's a good thing I baked a cake this morning. We'll serve it when Ted and his family come by this evening."

"Shall I take out these sliced tomatoes?" Helen asked Dora as she carried the large bowl of potatoes toward the back door.

"Yes, thank you. We're ready to eat."

As they gathered around the table, Mick led them in prayer.

"Our heavenly Father, we thank thee for this bountiful food you have set before us. We are thankful that our family has arrived safely from Nebraska. We ask that you watch over them as they make Oregon their home and help them find work. Amen."

John put potatoes and chicken on his plate and started to eat. He told Dora and Mick that they met Paul on the highway that morning and that he, Helen, Bill and Ella planned to return to Hood River to pick apples in ten days.

"I wondered where Paul was livin'. I knew he was in Oregon," Dora said. She passed the bread and butter to George and handed a drumstick to her oldest son.

"It's good you'll have work next month," Mick replied. He sipped his coffee from the saucer. "There's work for anyone who wants it in the hop fields starting tomorrow morning. There are also prunes to pick. There'll be plenty of work to keep you busy for the next few weeks." Mick passed the food down the table, making sure everyone had what they wanted. "Dora has rented a house for Mary and Harmon and we'll sort out the living arrangements for everyone later. We've moved the kids to the back porch so Mary and Harmon can use the second bedroom. Gesina can sleep in their room and the rest of you can sleep on the floor."

As they cleared the supper dishes, three cars drove into the yard with several people inside.

"The Kleens have arrived," Mick laughed as he walked to greet them. Mary and Harmon knew everyone and people were talking all at once. Soon the coffee and angel food cake were brought out, along with the apple pie, peach cobbler and fresh cream the Kleens brought.

George turned to his mother in bewilderment. "Who are all these people?" he asked.

"These are your relatives, my first cousins," Mary replied.

George scratched his head. He thought they'd left all their relatives in Nebraska, but the person who stopped to help them this morning was Uncle Paul, and when they drove into Salem and didn't know where to go, Ted Kleen, Ma's first cousin, was there to show them the way. Aunt Dora and Uncle Mick were here, also. He guessed that this was as much home as Nebraska had been. He took a bite of pie with fresh cream and sighed, content that family was here to greet him in Oregon.

The next morning everyone gathered around the table in Dora's kitchen. Dora was at the stove cooking the eggs and bacon, and Mary was toasting the bread.

"It sure got cold last night," John said as he drank some coffee. "The warmth of the stove feels good. Does it get cold like this every night through the summer?"

Mick took his plate of food from Dora. "When I got up the temperature was about forty- seven. It's been about that for the last week. It usually cools off at night here. It sure made short work of milking this morning with you, Bill, George and Harmon helping out."

"We'll help morning and night," Bill said. He started to eat the eggs Ella handed him. "We appreciate you putting us up."

"You girls put out all the dirty clothes," Dora said. "Mary and I will do the wash today."

"I have everything in a pile and I'll put it on the back porch. Thank you for doin' the wash." Helen wore the pair of overalls and the shirt and shoes she had brought with her. All the travelers except Mary and Gesina were going to work in the fields.

"I'll put ours there, too." Ella had borrowed overalls and a shirt from Dora.

Bill, Ella and George picked prunes and Harmon shook the prune trees. Harmon used a long pole with a hook on the end and when the hook was over a branch high in the tree he would push up and pull down several times until the prunes fell to the ground. The pickers would come along on their hands and knees and put the prunes into their buckets. Once a bucket was full they would dump it into a wooden box. Into each box they filled with prunes, they put a piece of paper with their name on it. Pickers were paid per box, but Harmon was paid by the hour.

John and Helen picked hops. The rows were narrow and the hops vines rose fifteen to twenty feet in the air. When they started on a row, the owner lowered the vines to the ground and the pickers, standing on the ground, would strip the hops into a basket. The hops were soft and green and smelled pleasant. Gloves and long sleeved shirts protected John and Helen from the abrasive vines. They were glad to have straw hats to protect them from the sun.

That night everyone sat at the supper table in the shade of the maple tree. "Dora helped me wash everyone's clothes, and we'll iron tomorrow," Mary said. "It sure felt good to be doin' something instead of riding in the car all day."

"My arms are tired from pulling down on those prune tree limbs." Harmon rubbed his elbows.

"I picked two-hundred boxes of prunes today." George rubbed the back of his legs. "My knees hurt."

"Well, I scooted around on my bottom part of the day," Ella said as everyone laughed. "I ate a lot of them, too; they are really good."

"Helen and I stood all day and could keep in the shade of the vines part of the time." John took a second helping of fried potatoes.

"George, you get paid four cents a box for the prunes. That means you made eight dollars today." Mick poured a second glass of milk for George.

George just sat there with his mouth open. "I can't believe it, eight dollars for one day's work? In Nebraska it would have taken me two and a half weeks to make eight dollars."

"Dora, this strawberry jam is wonderful," Helen said, spreading jam on her slice of bread. "Do strawberries grow around here?"

"Yes, strawberry season is at the end of May, for three or four weeks," Dora said.

"Well, I'm going to pick some next year and make jam," Helen nodded. "I did bring some chokecherry jam with me."

"Chokecherry jam." Dora's hazel eyes got dreamy. "That's my favorite jam, and I haven't had any for years."

"I'll get a jar for you after supper," Helen said.

Dora was silent for a moment. "Helen, I'll trade you – one of your jars of chokecherry jam for one of my jars of strawberry jam."

"That's just fine with me," Helen laughed. Each of them felt they got the better part of the bargain.

Picking prunes was only a two day job, but on the afternoon of the second day, Hersh, the owner, invited all the workers to his house for ice cream and cake and gave each person a $1.00 bonus for doing such a good job.

Bill, Ella, Gesina, Helen, George

AUGUST 30, 1934

August 30, 1934

Dear Mom and Dick,

I hope you received the short letter I sent to you when we arrived in Pratum. Everyone was relieved we were done traveling. I was sure glad your letter was waiting for me. It was wonderful hearing from you and knowing what is happening at home. When I opened your letter, Nebraska dust fell out.

Aunt Dora boarded and fed all eight of us for the first week. John and I, Bill and Ella slept on the floor but it was heaven after the hard ground and cement we'd put our thin mattresses on during our long trip out.

John and I had sixteen dollars left. We started out with seventy-five dollars. Bill and Ella started with forty dollars and had thirteen dollars left. We have all been picking prunes and hops and are working every day.

Gesina was ill for about five days after we arrived. She was worn out from traveling. Mick looked after her and said she probably didn't drink enough water on the trip. She is feeling much better and gaining weight. It's good to see her laughing again.

The Sunday after we arrived we all went to the coast. We went to Neskowin where there was a community kitchen, a large area with a roof and lots of wood stoves. Mick bought a salmon off a boat and Dora sliced it and fried it in the kitchen area. It was so good!

It was a long walk through the sand to the ocean, but the sun was shining although it was windy. We wore our jackets. We watched the waves roll, crash and send water onto the beach and spray onto us. We took off our shoes and socks and waded into the surf. Our feet quickly became numb from the cold water, but the sand felt warm between our toes. The Pacific Ocean is magnificent. I can't wait for you to see it.

I got carsick riding over the winding road to and from the beach. Oregon doesn't have roads like Nebraska, which are straight and cross at every section; these roads wander everywhere and have no rhyme or reason to them that I can see.

We like it here. It's warm and sunny but not too hot and the twilight stretches out until after 8 pm. It's great to be making money every day, and there's lots of food available. You need to come out and see for yourself.

I miss you both,

Love, Helen

John and Helen picking apples

SEPTEMBER 1934

The Hood River apple orchard covered many acres. The trees were tall and branches hung heavy with apples. Several branches were propped up with lumber to keep the limbs from breaking. It was quiet and the air was still. Helen listened to the birds as she picked the Red Delicious apples from the tree and carefully placed them in her bucket. She had a harness wrapped around her shoulders and back, and a hook on the front of the harness that attached to the bucket. She was on a ladder that had two long prongs which stuck into the ground, and the ladder rungs leaned against the tree. Above her, Johnny was on a taller ladder that had a narrow leg in the back that ran from the top of the ladder to the ground.

She stayed on one ladder rung and reached enough apples to fill her bucket, then she climbed down and carefully put the apples from her bucket into a box. She was careful not to dump the apples into the wooden box because she didn't want to bruise them. When she needed to move her ladder she would holler at Johnny and he would find another place for it. One day they picked one hundred boxes of apples off one huge tree, but normally the trees would produce enough apples to fill just twenty to forty boxes. They got paid four cents a box, so they made four dollars just from that tree. There were several different types of apples in the orchard – the yellow Newtown, Spitzenberg, Jonathan and Ortley, in addition to the Delicious.

In the tree beside them she could hear the murmur of Bill and Ella talking. The four of them had arrived in Hood River two days ago and rented a two-bed tourist cabin for four dollars and fifty cents for the three-week apple season. Besides the two beds there was a wood cook stove, a table and four chairs. They got water from the pump in the middle of the camp and used a common bathhouse. The outdoor toilets were behind the camp. They had brought food to make sandwiches and there were lots of fresh vegetables - green beans, tomatoes and corn - to buy from the fruit stand near the small grocery store.

Helen laughed to herself as she remembered a recent night when the manager of the camp had come knocking at their door telling them to be a little more quiet, as others were trying to sleep. *It's fun being with Bill and Ella,* she thought. *We laugh a lot and have lots of fun playing pinochle every evening.*

Johnny climbed down from his ladder and transferred his apples into a box. "Helen, are you ready for coffee?" he called.

Helen looked down and saw his blue eyes peering at her through the branches.

"I sure am." She climbed down from the ladder and unhooked her bucket from her body harness. She put her hands at the back of her hips and pushed her body forward, stretching her back. She pulled the sun-bonnet off her head and shook out her short, dark hair. "I'm glad we're working in the shade of the trees; at least it's a little cooler than working in the fields."

Bill and Ella joined them and they sat down under the tree and they each ate one of the cinnamon rolls that John had bought earlier that morning on the way to the orchard. They washed them down with cold coffee.

"Boy, this just hits the spot, doesn't it?" Ella said as she dusted cinnamon and sugar off her mouth.

Bill nodded. "John, you and Helen about done with that tree?"

"We have a ways to go yet. Are you done with yours?"

"Almost. When we get done, do you want us to help you finish up?"

"Thanks. That would be good."

Helen bent from the waist and touched her toes. "I'm sure glad I brought a pair of overalls with me from Nebraska."

Ella nodded. "I want to buy a couple pair for myself when we get enough money saved up, then I can give this pair back to Dora."

Bill took off his cap and wiped his face. "I noticed they have overalls for sale at the grocery store here. They're about the same price as in Nebraska."

The routine was set. They were in the orchard by eight in the morning and worked until about six at night. They took morning and afternoon breaks and ate the lunch the women had packed at noon. In the evening the men gathered wood from the woodpile by their cabin and the women fixed a hot meal of fried potatoes, a fresh vegetable and meat - either steak or chicken.

They had been picking apples for a few days when John looked down to see Paul standing at the base of the tree. "Hi Paul, how's things goin'?" John called.

"Doin' okay. Can you and Bill come down for a minute? I want to talk to ya."

John climbed down the ladder and put the apples into the half-filled box. He pushed his quilted cap to the back of his head and took a drink of water from the ladle Paul was holding out to him. Bill joined them.

Paul grinned. "The four of you are such good workers that Mr. Nichelson wants all four of ya to report to the packing shed in the morning."

"What would we do there?" Bill asked as he wiped his head with his handkerchief.

"There are different jobs, and I don't know what he will have you men do, but the women will probably work on the belt sorting apples."

The next morning Helen and Ella sorted and packed apples earning twenty cents an hour. John and Bill earned thirty cents an hour by carefully emptying the boxes of apples onto a wide belt that kept moving past the women on the line.

As the apples continued down the moving belt, they were washed and then polished with a brush. The fruit kept moving down the belt and dropped by sizes into the appropriate bins, sorting extra fancy, fancy and C-grade. At the end of the line, women carefully handpacked the apples into shipping boxes. The apples were shipped immediately by train or sent to cold storage.

One morning Helen decided to bake bread to surprise the men, but the dough didn't rise and she had to throw it into the garbage can.

"I'll make it tomorrow," Ella said as she cleaned the table after supper. "You must have just forgotten some ingredient."

"I don't think I left anything out." Helen washed the dishes in a big tub and dipped them in another tub of water to rinse them. Then she handed them to John who dried them.

"Ella makes really great bread," Bill leaned back on his chair.

"So does Helen," John grinned at Helen. "She's never had a problem before."

The next morning Ella mixed up the dough and it was even worse than Helen's batch. Ella threw the dough away and it made a bigger dent in the garbage can than Helen's.

When Ella and Helen were at the grocery store the next time Helen noticed there were two types of flour on the shelf. "What's the difference between the two types of flour?" she asked the grocer.

"You use soft wheat flour to make cakes and the hard wheat flour for everything else." When Helen got back to the cabin she checked the sack of flour and it was the soft wheat flour, not the kind used for making bread. In Nebraska they only had hard wheat flour that they used for everything.

At the end of the harvest, both couples had made seventy-five dollars. They felt rich.

Helen and John 1935

FALL 1934 THROUGH SPRING 1935

The house Aunt Dora had rented for Harmon and Mary was close to their place. One Sunday in early November, after church services at the Pratum Methodist church, the family gathered for dinner at Harmon and Mary's. Helen and Ella were setting the table in the dining room.

"I sure like the people at the Methodist church. I think John Olthoff would make a wonderful husband for my mom. I hope she comes out soon so she can meet him." Helen wore the dress she had been married in and her gray pumps.

"John Olthoff? Isn't he the one that was married to Mary's cousin Lydia, who died?" Ella also wore her wedding dress and the blue skirt of the dress swirled around her ankles.

"Yes, she was his second wife. I guess his first wife ran off with a sailor."

"Really! So that means he was divorced. I don't think I've known anyone who's been divorced. He's such a handsome man, I doubt he will stay single long," Ella said.

"Probably not. Ella, how are things going for you and Bill?" Helen asked as she flipped the tablecloth across the table.

"Uncle Mick made arrangements for us to work for Mr. Emery, the farmer who lives just down the road. He pays us fifteen dollars a month with room and board. I help around the house and with the cooking, and Bill helps on the farm." Ella grabbed the other side of the tablecloth and helped Helen spread it on the table. "But Bill has found us a better job working for Harry Riches on his farm. We start there next month. I'll earn two bits an hour doing housework for a neighbor. We've rented a little house for four dollars a month, and it will be just the two of us."

Helen smiled. "That would be nice, to have your own house instead of living with someone else."

Ella's eyes crinkled up and she laughed. "Actually this will be the first time just the two of us have lived together. When I was teaching school we had to live apart and after school was out we lived with Bill's folks. I imagine we'll have some adjustments to make."

Gesina walked into the room with an armful of plates. She had gained back some weight, but was still very thin. "Here are the plates," she made a face. "I have to sit at the kitchen table with the little kids."

Helen took the plates from Gesina and started placing them on the table.

"I'm sorry you have to be in the kitchen, but with Mick and Dora here there isn't room for everyone at the dining room table." The aroma of sauerkraut and wieners drifted into the room. "Mm, that sure smells good. Is that some of the sauerkraut that Dora made?"

"Yes, she gave Ma a crock of it," Gesina said as she went to the kitchen to get the silverware.

"Harmon and Mary were sure lucky to get such nice furniture at the auction. This table is beautiful," Ella said. "I guess we'll go to the auction to get our furniture when we move into the house."

"Gesina, how is school going?" Helen helped Gesina place silverware at each plate.

"Willard School is alright, and it's nearby, just outside Pratum, but I miss my school in Nebraska. I was going to start the fifth grade with my friends." Gesina wore the blue print dress that Aunt Dora had helped Mary make. Today a white bib apron covered the dress.

"I like your dress. It brings out the blue in your eyes." Helen gave Gesina a hug. "I know you miss your friends. I really miss my mom and brother, and it will be very hard over the holidays not to have them around, especially Thanksgiving and Christmas."

"I miss my family, too," Ella replied. They were quiet for a moment, each lost in their thoughts of home. Ella shook her head and started placing glasses around the table. "Helen, are you still working for Mrs. Thompson?"

"Yes, Aunt Dora found the job for me. I live at the house with Mrs. Thompson. I stay with her mother during the day and fix her lunch. I also clean the house and help fix the other meals. Johnny spends the night with me, but eats all of his meals at his parents'."

"Are Harmon, George and John still cutting wood?"

'Yes, they keep busy. Various people want them to help get their woodpiles ready for winter." Helen brushed the front of her dress with her hand. "Oh, I forgot to tell you. Two weeks ago Mrs. Butler, another neighbor, asked if I would come help with the housework when their son Robert was born. I stayed at their house for a week. The first night I stayed there Johnny came to visit and we stayed in the kitchen. The next morning Mrs. Butler told me to bring Johnny in the front room and let them visit with him, too. Mrs. Butler paid me five dollars for the week."

"That's great," Ella said. "Then did you go back to Mrs. Thompson's?"

"Yes, she still needs help with her mom. It seems that just as one job finishes for Johnny or me someone else hires us. The good part is that we keep making money." Helen looked around her. "Isn't fall a beautiful season here?" The trees - maple, oak and birch - were dropping their colorful leaves. "There are so many bright colors, yellow, orange, and red. It takes my breath away."

"They are beautiful, but I don't like raking them," Gesina said, putting her arms around Helen's waist.

Helen hugged her back.

"Girls," Mary hollered, "is the table ready?"

"Yes," they replied in unison as they went to the kitchen to help dish up the food.

* * * * *

In one of her letters to her mother that winter, Helen wrote: *Mom, you need to come and see us, you could ride the train. There is a gentleman here I want you to meet. I think he would make a good husband for you. His name is John Olthoff. He's short, fat, and bald. No, no, just kidding. He's tall, slender and has a beautiful head of hair.*

I think of you so often, and miss you.

* * * * *

"Helen, you're going to like Dr. Loar's place in the Silverton Hills." John drove the Ford Tudor east out of Silverton. The car was loaded with all of their clothes and other belongings.

"Dr. Loar has a small sawmill where people work on Saturdays to pay off their medical bills," John continued. "Besides taking care of the animals, I'll cut down trees and haul the logs to the mill. As I told you before, he'll pay us thirty dollars a month and the best part is we will get to live in the house on the property."

"What's the house like?" Helen asked as she looked out the window. The spring flowers were more beautiful than the fall leaves. There were tulips, daffodils, and crocuses. The rhododendron bushes bloomed with red, pink and white flowers.

"I haven't seen it yet, but Mick said it was a nice place." John shifted into second gear as the car started the climb into the hills. "You'll help raise turkeys. Dr. Loar expects to send one hundred turkeys to market this year. We'll get to use the eggs from the chickens and the milk from the cow. Dr. Loar said we could eat the chickens and when he butchers a steer in a few weeks he'll share the meat with us."

John stopped the car in front of the garage. John and Helen put on their boots and, holding hands, they walked around the barnyard looking at the chickens and turkeys. In the nearby pasture they could see the white-faced cattle and a Jersey cow.

The white house on Dr. Loar's farm was built against the hillside and had a yard around it. There was a kitchen, living room, two bedrooms and a bathroom.

"The house is wonderful," Helen called. "Have you seen the indoor toilet and bathtub? How do we heat the water for the tub? And how do they get running water? Just think. I won't have to use a hand pump to get water."

"The water is piped from a spring above the house," John said, turning on a faucet in the kitchen. "The hot water line runs through the wood stove." His blue eyes crinkled with excitement.

"I don't mind not having electricity; we can use the Aladdin lamp." Helen looked at the lamp sitting on the table. "There's a lamp in the living room, too. It's really nice that the house has all this furniture. We won't have to buy anything."

"Let's get the car unloaded and I'll check on the livestock." John walked toward the back door.

"Okay, and then I'll get supper started. It sure is a nice place," Helen said. Then she called, "Johnny."

John stopped and looked at her. "What?"

"I'm so glad that it's just the two of us. It seems like forever since we've lived in a house of our own."

John nodded. "Yes, our living arrangements have been pretty mixed up these last six or seven months. It's good to be together with no one else here."

One Sunday they packed a picnic lunch and went to Silver Creek Falls. They walked down to the waterfall below the picnic area. The trail was muddy and slick with sharp drop-offs and they carefully helped each other along. The forest floor was covered with ferns, moss and wildflowers. They walked behind the large waterfall and could feel the misty spray as they looked through the sheets of water falling from above.

"Let's come back in the summer and walk some of the trails to see the other waterfalls," Helen said as she looked at her reflection in the pool at the bottom of the falls.

"Yeah. We can have everyone come with us and have a family picnic," John agreed.

They liked living at Dr. Loar's place. It was beautiful in the woods, all lush and green. It would rain for days or even weeks at a time, but they didn't mind.

When John didn't need Jack, the horse, to haul lumber, Helen would ride him. The farm dog, Sam, would follow along. They spent a lot of time wandering among the gorgeous fir trees.

"Helen," John said the first morning she started out on the horse, "stay near the railroad track so you don't get lost. But if you do wander off the track, just let Jack have his head and he'll come home."

One day, when Helen was lying on the ground looking up at the tall fir trees, Jack and Sam both started acting real nervous. Jack pawed the ground and whinnied while Sam was running toward the bushes and barking. Helen got on the horse and left as quickly as she could because Johnny had said there were bears around and she was afraid one was nearby.

That night at supper Helen told John about being scared in the woods. "Do you think it was a bear?" she asked.

"Could have been; they're probably waking up from their winter sleep. Just be careful and pay attention to Sam and the horse."

"Okay," Helen replied. "Johnny, when I was in Nebraska I used to wonder where they got trees tall and straight enough for the poles that carried the electric lines through the countryside. I've found those trees in Oregon."

John laughed. "Yeah, they could use some of these trees I'm cutting down for telephone poles."

The house sat about halfway up a hill and at the bottom of the hill was Powers Creek. They dammed it up and made a swimming hole, but they only splashed around because the water was cold and neither of them knew how to swim.

One evening after supper, John and Helen were sitting under the maple tree enjoying the evening. "It's nice to have it light so late, isn't it?" Helen sighed.

"Yep, and it's almost time for bed." Yawning, John put his arm around Helen. "I need to haul a lot of logs to the mill tomorrow." After a moment he added, "We did good, didn't we, coming to Oregon?"

"Yes. We've both been able to find work and we've even saved up a little money. I know we couldn't have done that in Nebraska. There's such an abundance of food here. I'm really looking forward to the strawberries, raspberries and boysenberries. Then there will be the garden crops - beans, tomatoes, corn and potatoes. And at the end of the summer there will be peaches and pears to pick. Won't it be wonderful! I'll be able to can everything this summer and then we'll have lots of food to use this winter."

"If things continue on so well, we'll be able to buy a farm within a few years."

"Wouldn't that be wonderful," Helen's eyes looked off into the distance and she snuggled into the crook of John's arm. "A farm would be a great place to raise a family."

John smiled at her. "Yeah. Well, let's just wait awhile."

Helen laughed back at him. "Okay, we'll wait awhile."

John stood up and stretched, then reached down and pulled Helen to her feet. Heads together and arms around each other, they walked toward the house.

Helen slowly opened her eyes. She was in her apartment at Applewood Retirement Home in Salem where she had lived for the past eight years. She stretched and rubbed her eyes. The clock chimed 4:30 pm.

She felt happy; must have been her dream about their trip to Oregon. That first year of marriage had a lot of big changes for her, Johnny and the rest of the Schafer family. The only ones still alive who made the trip besides her were Ella and Gesina. *We're all three widows*, she thought.

She laid her head back on the chair and thought about their life in Oregon. Johnny started work at the Reid and Murdock cannery in Salem during the summer of 1935. After the cannery season ended each fall, she and Johnny returned to pick apples in Hood River for the next few years. He started working year-round at the cannery in 1942.

It was 1936 when Elmer, her oldest brother, drove to Oregon, pulling a trailer with all the items that they had left behind. *It was so good to have all our things with us.* Helen smiled when she saw the four remaining long-stemmed green water glasses that had been a wedding gift sitting in her hutch. After World War II, Elmer moved his family to Oregon. They lived in Independence for four years where he owned a filling station, but he returned to the military and made it his life's career.

Helen stretched her arms above her head and yawned. The move to Oregon was good for everyone. She ran her arthritic fingers through her white hair and chuckled as she thought about all the people that had followed them to Oregon.

In the summer of 1935, Ella was picking strawberries when she looked up and saw her father walking toward her. He had driven to Oregon to see what it had to offer. Ella's parents, Paul and Pauline Scharff, and Ella's sister and brother-in-law, Augusta and Johnny Scharff, moved to Oregon in 1936 and settled in Silverton. Ella and Bill lived at various locations in Salem. They were involved in the development of several golf courses around the Salem area. They had one son. They celebrated seventy-one years of marriage before Bill passed in 2004.

Harmon and Mary lived in Pratum for three years, then in Wheatland, where Harmon worked on a dairy. They finally settled in the Hazel Green area where Mary worked as a janitor for the Hazel Green Grade School. They were married for fifty-nine years.

Gesina was sixteen the first time she saw Grover Lichty. She rode along with Bill when he went to the blacksmith shop in Central Howell to get a part for his mower. Grover was working for the blacksmith. Shortly thereafter Gesina went to the Waldo Hill pie social and square dance with her family, and Grover asked her to dance. She had just turned seventeen when they got married and they raised their three children in Central Howell, near Pratum. In 1948 Grover started his own blacksmith business. They were married for fifty-nine years when Grover died, in 1998.

Before George left to serve in World War II, he married Afton Barnes. They had one son. They farmed in West Salem and in Hopewell, then moved to Wemme, on Mt. Hood, where he was greens keeper at the Wemme golf course. After he retired, they moved to Salem. They had been married sixty-three years in 2001, when Afton preceded George in death by three months.

Helen smiled, thinking about how her mom had ridden the train out to visit. After Lurena met John Olthoff, she returned to Kearney and sold her farm. She moved to Oregon and married John. They lived in various homes in the Salem area and were married for thirty-six years. Lurena was ninety-seven when she died.

Dick, who stayed in Kearney to finish his senior year of high school, came to Oregon in 1938 and for two years worked in Klamath Falls at a sawmill. Dick eventually settled in California where he raised his family.

Bob, Helen's other brother, moved to Oregon in 1939, married Eunice Laughlin and raised his two girls in Salem.

Uncle Tom Marshall, who fed her and Johnny a hamburger at the beginning of their trip at the Hamburger Hut in Cozad, moved to Oregon within a few years and lived in Roberts, south of Salem.

And there was Johnny's younger cousin, Herman Wilken and his wife, Marie, who came to Oregon a few years later and raised their family in Salem.

Helen remembered all the times that Uncle Paul came to the farm and Johnny would always have money to give him. Paul never did settle down in one job or place.

Helen stretched again and looked out the window. The fir tree branches were swaying softly in the breeze. She and Johnny had made such a good life. They bought a farm in the Middle Grove area east of Salem in 1942, where they raised their three children. It was a nice community and the grade school was only a mile from the farm. They always had cows, chickens, and pigs. She laughed as she saw herself clearing the electric fence when the sow chased her out of the pasture. They paid for the farm by raising and selling a litter of pigs quarterly each year. When the post office changed the address from route and box numbers, the neighbors asked to have the street named Schafer Avenue.

In the fall of 1944, she and Johnny and the kids made their first trip back to Nebraska to visit family and friends. They were gone for a month. *I'm so glad we came to Oregon. It was the right thing for us to do. I was shocked at how dry and dusty it still was there. I guess I'd gotten used to Oregon's lush forests and abundant crops. And it was so cold. Our winters are much milder,* she thought.

When Johnny retired, they sold the farm and moved about a mile across the way to the new house on 48th Avenue N.E. John retired at age sixty-two from U. S. Products, the same cannery he started at in 1935, but with a different name. While they were never rich, they were comfortable in their lifestyle. *We were very happy together, but there were dark times also.* Helen felt her body tense and tears gathered in her eyes. They had just celebrated forty-nine years of marriage when she and Johnny went fishing on opening day at Detroit Lake. They had been drifting in the boat and when Johnny tried to start the engine it just sputtered and died. He pulled the engine up to check it and when the engine dropped back into place Johnny flew into the water. He didn't know how to swim. She was unable to save him and had to watch him go under. She endured three dark years until his body was recovered. Once he was buried, she was able to move forward in her life, but unable to leave her grief behind. She took a deep breath. She had been without him for twenty-two years and sometime soon she would leave her pain-ridden body behind and be ready to go to him with open arms.

But not now, now it was time for supper.

EPILOGUE

The old highway between Mosier and Hood River isn't accessible by car and the Mosier Twin Tunnels, built in 1921, are located in this section. At one time the Twin Tunnels were one of the marvels of the Scenic Columbia Gorge. Although the tunnels were narrow they could easily accommodate two-way traffic by Model A's in 1934, but as cars became larger, accidents were common. In the 1950's the tunnels were closed and filled with rock and remained that way until they were restored as part of a hiking and bicycling path, in 1995.

On May 25, 2006, Gary, my husband, and today our chauffer, drops my daughter, Sarah, and I off at the west trailhead, just outside of Hood River, to walk the Twin Tunnels. The sign at the start of the trail indicates it is 4.6 miles to the east trailhead located just west of Mosier where Gary will pick us up.

As we walk I see the shadows of the two-car, one-truck caravan that brought my family to Oregon over this route in 1934. Today we walk in the opposite direction than the way my family drove, but I turn backwards often to see the view they saw. It would have been late afternoon on August 19, 1934, when they passed through here and I try to imagine the way the shadows of the trees would have splayed across the narrow road.

We walk about an hour before we start the downhill grade that leads into the tunnels. Just before the tunnels, a large turn-out area on the north side of the road overlooks the Columbia River. I picture the 1930 Ford Tudor, the 1928 Oldsmobile Whippet and the old truck parked in that turn-out and my dad, my uncles and my grandfather standing around the truck pouring water into the steaming radiator while my mother, aunt and grandmother lean against the stone wall, embracing the breeze and drinking in the beautiful view of the Columbia Gorge.

The inside of the west tunnel has been reinforced with timber but the east tunnel still has rock forming the curve of the ceiling. There are two portals that let light into the east tunnel. One of the portals used to lead to a cliff-side walkway on the outside of the tunnel so the beauty of the Columbia River Gorge could be viewed in all its glory. These portals are now crumbling rocks and fenced off for safety. Once more I imagine the caravan driving through the tunnel and enjoying the coolness it offered.

Sarah and I leave the tunnel and amble down the old road, enjoying the sunshine and the view of the river. Continuing downhill we see Gary in the distance waiting for us, and I say goodbye to the ghosts of those family members who came before us when they moved to Oregon to find a better life.

I thank them for the gifts they brought with them and passed on to me, my children and my grandchildren: strong work ethics, strong family values and the willingness to take a calculated risk.